To Eric,
    With best wishes for
a joyous Christmas
and a happy, healthy 2006!
    Love,
        Jasmine

December 2005

Mikhail Zoshchenko
A Man
Is Not
A Flea

STORIES

Translated by Serge Shishkoff

Ardis, Ann Arbor

Mikhail Zoshchenko, *A Man Is Not a Flea*
Copyright © 1989 by Ardis Publishers
All rights reserved under International and Pan-American Copyright Conventions.
Printed in the United States of America

Ardis Publishers
2901 Heatherway
Ann Arbor, Michigan 48104

Library of Congress Cataloging-in-Publication Data

Zoshchenko, Mikhail, 1895-1958
[Short stories, English. Selections]
A man is not a flea: a collection of stories/by Mikhail
Zoshchenko; translated by Serge Shishkoff.
p. cm.
Translated from the Russian.
ISBN 0-87501-023-7 (alk. paper)
1. Zoshchenko, Mikhail, 1895-1958—Translations, English.
I. Title.
PG3476.Z7A27   1989
891.73'42—dc20   89-661
CIP

CONTENTS

Acknowledgments 7
Foreword 9

The Electrician 21
The Dictaphone 23
The Barrel 26
A Halloween Story 28
Bathhouse 31
Lemonade 34
An Aristocratic Lady 36
The Actor 40
Adventure Movie 43
Happiness 45
A Dog's Nose 48
A Lamentable Incident 51
Thieves 53
The Charms of Civilization 55
Frazzled Nerves 59
Westinghouse Brake 62
Shortage 64
Of Cats and Men 67
Insufficient Packaging 69
Firewood 73
Quality Goods 76
Penal Servitude 79
"No Waste" Campaign 82
The Cup 84
The Passenger 87
Four Days 90
The Bathhouse vs. the People 92
The Adventures of a Monkey 96
The Terrible Night 104
What the Nightingale Sang about 121

Acknowledgments

I wish to express my sincere gratitude to my wife, Olga, who patiently edited, corrected, and criticized my translations and who, with angelic forbearance, endured my frequent petulant displays of resentment at having my work found to be less than perfect.

I also wish to thank all of my colleagues, and in particular Natalie Challis, Mark Suino, and Irwin Titunik, for their generous help and encouragement.

Foreword

1

When I was a youngster in a small town in Yugoslavia during the Second World War, my parents' friends—other Russian émigrés—often gathered at our house. Sometimes, after the usual tea and chitchat about weather and politics, someone produced a dog-eared volume of Zoshchenko's stories in a cheap Riga[1] edition and began reading from it. Obviously everybody knew these stories almost by heart, since chuckles of anticipation could be heard after the first sentence or two. With every following sentence, laughter grew in intensity until, toward the end of the story, all the listeners were literally doubled over with laughter, tears streaming down their faces, barely able to breathe. The reader frequently had to interrupt his reading to join in the general merriment, wipe the tears from his eyes and recover his composure. Although I probably missed half of what was funny, I too laughed—often by contagion, no doubt—as hard as I have ever laughed since. It was the memory of these cheerful moments in the otherwise dreadful times in occupied Yugoslavia that provided me with the impetus to undertake the arduous task of translating Zoshchenko into English.

2

Zoshchenko was, I dare say, the most subversive of Soviet writers. The funny thing is, he got away with it for some twenty-five years, surviving the bloody purges of the 1930s and avoiding the fate of so many of his literary contemporaries whose entries in the *Brief Literary Encyclopedia* end with the grim laconic remarks "illegally repressed" and "posthumously rehabilitated." Also ironic is the fact that when the Soviet authorities did go after him in 1946, they seemed to miss the point entirely, for, as the *pièce de résistance* in their case against him, they used the most innccuous story, "The Adventures of a Monkey" (included in this collection for this reason), to prove that Zoshchenko was slandering the Soviet people.

Zoshchenko began to write right after the Bolshevik Revolution, at the time when the new Soviet government was faced with enormous tasks. The country, devastated by the recent upheavals, had to be rebuilt, public institutions, swept away by the revolution, had to be reestablished, relations with foreign countries had to be normalized, and so on. But the most important and, as it turned out, the most difficult task was transforming the backward, ignorant, and bewildered Russian masses into worthy citizens of the new socialist state. A vast campaign of exhortation, education, and, not infrequently, coercion was launched to produce, practically overnight, the new Soviet man. As envisioned by the authorities, this creature would be boundlessly and selflessly devoted to the collective, would work unstintingly to the full extent of his abilities on the building of the new society, would be free of the usual human failings and weaknesses, would be well educated and politically and socially sophisticated. Writers were asked, more and more insistently as time went on and the new regime became more secure and better organized, to participate in this effort by writing about the future proletarian heroes and the future splendid life for the edification of the masses. (This type of writing eventually became institutionalized under the Kafkaesque name "Socialist Realism"). In those heady, optimistic times, the government believed that it would take maybe two or three years to achieve this goal (that, at least, is the impression one gets when reading the pronouncements made at the time).

It was against this background that in 1921 Mikhail Zoshchenko appeared on the literary scene with his stories and quickly bacame immensely popular. But Zoshchenko was a satirist, and satirists cannot be made to lie in the procrustean bed of programmatic literature. They must write about what they see before their eyes, and what Zoshchenko saw was the usual assortment of deadly and lesser sins. While each of Zoshchenko's stories could be viewed (and was) as an attack on the vestiges of bourgeois mentality, on the survival of pre-revolutionary attitudes, and generally on social and psychological factors impeding the rapid development of "homo sovieticus," the cumulative effect of the stories is quite different. For one thing, it soon becomes apparent that Zoshchenko's satire transcends any such narrow classification. Like all great satirists since Aesop, Zoshchenko castigates the sins and foibles that are typical for humans in every society and at all times, including the USSR after the Revolution. For another, Zoshchenko, while deploring these failings and holding them up for ridicule, has a profound sympathy, respect, even love, for his, to say the least, imperfect heroes.

Party officials soon sensed that Zoshchenko's stories were seditious and started attacking him with increasing ferocity. Being a satirist has always been a high-risk occupation in Russia, but under the humorless, dour Marxist-Leninist leadership endowed with self-proclaimed infallibility it was tantamount to suicide. Still, up to about 1928, literature in the USSR enjoyed considerable freedom. Groupings of writers with varying political and aesthetic views coexisted (though not altogether peacefully), lively exchanges of views on literary and other topics were carried out in a relatively large number of journals which were not yet under complete government control, much valuable scholarly work outside the officially sanctioned Marxist-Leninist orientation (up to a point, of course) was published, and public debates on a wide variety of issues were held. During this period Zoshchenko was recognized as a major writer, his works were regularly published in large editions, articles and even books by some of the most eminent literary critics and scholars of the time (Shklovsky, Vinogradov, and others) analyzed various aspects of his work and, between 1929 and 1931, a complete collection of Zoshchenko's works in six volumes was published.

Around 1927 (this was a gradual process, so it is impossible to set a precise date) the government began to formulate and enforce a set of rules for Soviet writers. Also it gradually assumed control of all publishing in the country and so could make it impossible for writers it deemed unworthy to publish their works. After about 1930 it applied even sterner measures against them. Yet, for various reasons, including, one suspects, uncommon cleverness on Zoshchenko's part, the authorities could do little to Zoshchenko besides accusing him of lacking a proper forward-looking spirit and using bad language.

Perhaps the best illustration of the difficulties the authorities had in dealing with Zoshchenko is the fact that in 1939 he was awarded a decoration "for outstanding contributions to Soviet literature" (or something like that), and another one in 1946, just a few months before he was denounced by Zhdanov as a renegade and declared to be a "cosmopolite," a "hooligan," and a few other choice things, and then made a non-person.

There were some obvious reasons for Zoshchenko's ability to survive. First of all, his popularity with readers was enormous. He was one of the most widely read writers of the period. Second, in his public life, Zoshchenko was conspicuously pro-Soviet. In the Civil War he had fought with the Red Army, and afterwards, especially in the 1930s, actively supported the goals the Communist Party had set for Soviet writers. He became a high official in the All-Russian Union of Soviet Writers, wrote many topical *feuilletons* to promote the aims of the First Five-Year Plan, and even participated in the infamous Belomorsk Canal project. He also wrote many pieces designed to show that he was "consonant with the epoch" as they liked to say in those days, such as his moralistic children's stories, his very orthodox stories about Lenin, tales about the partisans during World War II, etc. It is hard to tell whether he wrote all this for the purpose of self-preservation, or whether he really believed that it was a Soviet writer's duty to serve as a propagandist for the regime, but one thing is certain: these stories are far inferior to the "real" Zoshchenko's stories. Most of these, it should be noted, were written during the relatively free period, in the early and mid-20s. It is also noteworthy that soon after the Revolution Zoshchenko joined the Serapion Brothers group whose avowed purpose was to be apolitical and cultivate the art of writing good literature for its own sake.

It can be said, then, that his output falls into two categories: the quintessentially Zoshchenkovian works with their many-layered satire and their inimitable style, and the works that to one degree or another followed the prescriptions of the literary establishment. But Zoshchenko was so much more clever than the official critics who formulated those prescriptions that occasionally he was able to baffle them by writing ostensibly "orthodox" pieces which, on closer examination, turned out to be nothing of the sort. The best example of such slyness is undoubtedly his *Youth Restored* (1933). It purported to apply the scientific method to literature—something that cannot fail to appeal to any naive Marxist—and the authorities swallowed it hook, line, and sinker. Serious public discussions were held with the participation of eminent scientists, articles were written in scholarly journals—the whole thing became something of a *cause célèbre*. Yet now, in retrospect, it seems clear that it was all an elaborate hoax.[2]

As stated earlier, Zoshchenko did not write about idealized future proletarian heroes. The typical Zoshchenko hero was a little man, an ignorant, narrow-minded, and coarse "man in the street" whose universe was dominated by his efforts to survive, to pick up the threads of his life scattered by the recent cataclysmic events, to satisfy his philistine cravings, to cope with the multitude of trivial daily problems which, in those chaotic times, had a way of assuming epic proportions, and, most important, to stay out of the trouble that seemed to lurk around every corner. These efforts were made infinitely more difficult by the necessity to adapt himself to new circumstances, new language, new institutions and new social relations. Most of this was well above his head, and his hero's pitiful attempts to adjust to the new life were a major source of Zoshchenko's humor. This "hero" picked up some of the new political jargon without understanding what it meant, learned, usually not quite correctly, some of the revolutionary slogans while being only dimly aware of the realities behind them, and so he usually missed the point, did the wrong thing, and got in trouble. Yet, every morning he got up full of cheerful optimism, hoping to find an apartment—something he had been trying to do for the last six months, or get washed in a public bathhouse, or recover his overshoes, or have his stove fixed.

Zoshchenko's stories are usually told from the point of view of a narrator who is indistinguishable from the characters in the story. This method of narration is, on one hand, a clever ploy putting the critical Party officials in an awkward position. Since the author's voice is never heard directly (well... hardly ever) and the stories are so subtly and cleverly written, the authorities found it extremely difficult to define Zoshchenko's ideological position in order to attack it. Whenever they objected to anything in a story, he could very reasonably answer that one cannot hold a writer accountable for what his fictional characters do or say. On the other hand, the device of telling the story from the point of view of an unreliable narrator (*skaz*) gave Zoshchenko endless oportunity for humor and satire. Also, one cannot help but realize that by means of this device Zoshchenko identifies himself with his characters. It becomes clear that Zoshchenko is on their side, that he accepts them such as they are, and, while deploring their shortcomings, he demands respect for them because they are human beings—and a human being is much more than any list of qualities, good or bad, that those currently in power may compile. This alone is enough to make Zoshchenko subversive, since the Soviet Government believes that a citizen is subservient to the state, while Zoshchenko, in the Western humanistic tradition, wants the government to be the servant of the people.

Furthermore, Zoshchenko believed that it is not possible to change human nature by decree. An individual may outwardly adopt the characteristics of the "new" personality, but beneath this veneer there will still be the unchanged, fallible human being who has withstood countless changes of regimes, repeated attempts to mold him into one shape or another, and the concerted efforts of satirists of all ages to make him see the error of his ways. It will take a profound change in human spirit and psychology to produce a better society, Zoshchenko keeps saying over and over again, and such a change takes a long time. One way Zoshchenko makes this point is by making explicit or implicit comparisons with the past or by projecting into the future ("Weak Packaging," "Happiness," "No Waste Campaign," "What the Nightingale Sang about," and others). It should be noted, though, that in a certain broad sense the wishes of the Soviet government and Zoshchenko coincided. They both hoped that brotherly love, unselfishness, and high spiritual values would replace the crass lower middle-class interests of the typical Zoshchenkovian character and his real-life prototype.

Zoshchenko's belief that it takes a long time to change human nature runs counter to the official Soviet credo that a change in political and social conditions will automatically and in short order produce a new and improved human being. What is more, Zoshchenko's view detracts from the importance of the Great October Revolution, which the Soviets have elevated to the status of a Myth of Creation. Zoshchenko reduces it to nothing more than another disturbance along the path of human betterment, which, Zoshchenko never fails to emphasize, comes from within, from the soul, and not in response to external factors.

In "What the Nightingale Sang about" Zoshchenko (or, more accurately, the narrator, although a good case can be made out that in this story the narrator is Zoshchenko himself) suggests that it may take "three hundred years or even less" to bring about "that splendid life." It is interesting that Zoshchenko chose that particular figure as it brings to mind the well-known statement Chekhov made in one of his more optimistic moments to the effect that things may get better in two hundred years or so. Is Zoshchenko saying that the revolution has set progress back by a hundred years?

Be that as it may, it is clear that the authorities found such statements most irksome. In the above-mentioned story, Zoshchenko goes on to say: "The author doesn't know and doesn't intend to venture guesses about the kind of life they'll have. Why on earth should the author frazzle his nerves and upset his health? There is no point in it whatsoever, since he will never see any of that splendid life anyway?"[3] But the editors or censors found it necessary to modify the passage as follows: "...There is no point in it whatsoever, since he will *probably* never see *all* of that splendid life anyway."[4] (Italics mine. S.Sh.)

3

The Revolution caused great changes in the Russian language. The mixing of social classes, the usual revolutionary contempt for the intellectuals and their elaborate language, the fact that people with little education ascended to positions of power (and felt compelled to use language in ways that far exceeded their competence), the avalanche of new political jargon and sloganeering, and the changed conditions of life in general produced a special brand of Russian characteristic of the 1920s. Zoshchenko, with his keen writer's ear, caught the spirit of that new lingo and, after concentrating it, giving it a satirical charge, and stylizing it, adopted it for use in his stories.

Superficially, Zoshchenko's language appears impoverished. It isn't. On the contrary, it is a very rich language, but Zoshchenko deliberately creates the illusion of inarticulateness and paucity. For instance, he saturates his dialogues with "I said," "he said," to the point of absurdity. There may be two or three of these per sentence. He also generally eschews synonyms, and uses the same word over and over again. His sentences, for the most part, are very short and frequently incomplete, and they begin, as often as not, with "and" or "but." His syntax is often mangled, and the grammar unpredictable.

His lexicon is a grotesque mixture of styles, from pompous political pronouncements (often satirically corrupted) and revolutionary slogans (usually comically misunderstood), to crass vulgarisms typical of the man in the street.[5] His adjectives clash with the nouns, the verbs are unexpectedly inappropriate, there are all kinds of malapropisms everywhere. All this adds up to a special, immediately recognizable Zoshchenkovian language and also makes his stories particularly well-suited for oral rendition. Indeed, variety shows throughout the 1920s featured readings of Zoshchenko's stories (sometimes by Zoshchenko himself) on their programs, always to the delight of the audiences.

This peculiar Zoshchenkovian idiom[6] is very difficult to translate as there are no English equivalents for many "Zoshchenkovianisms" and I am afraid that in many instances I have not been able to do Zoshchenko justice. It would practically have been necessary to invent a new English dialect for this purpose. But then could the resulting text be legitimately called a translation? This is the translator's dilemma at its worst. It is curious to note, incidentally, that Damon Runyon's English bears a certain superficial resemblance to Zoshchenko's Russian.

4

Important dates:

1895   Zoshchenko was born in Poltava. His father was an artist, his mother an actress.

1914   He joined the Russian Army as a volunteer. He served with distinction, was wounded and poisoned with gas.

1917-20   Years of wandering. Zoshchenko worked at many jobs. Served in the Red Army for a time.

1921   Settled in Leningrad (then still Petrograd) and began to write.

1922-c.1930   Zoshchenko wrote most of his best works. At the same time his relations with the authorities gradually worsened.

1929-31   The complete collection of Zoshchenko's works in 6 volumes was published in Moscow.

1931-40   Zoshchenko attempted to accommodate the authorities and adapt himself to Socialist Realism. He wrote feuilletons, stories about Kerenski, Lenin, moralistic children's tales. Travelled to factories, constructions sites, etc. He lead a very active public life. Nevertheless he was subject to increasing criticism from the establishment.

1933   Published *Youth Restored*.

1934-35   Wrote *The Blue Book*.

1938-39   Wrote the play *Dangerous Connections*.

1941-45   The war years. Zoshchenko wrote mostly patriotic stories about soldiers and partisans.

1943   Began publishing *Before Sunrise*.

1946   A.A. Zhdanov, a member of the Politbureau, viciously denounced Zoshchenko (along with Anna Akhmatova). As a result, Zoshchenko was thrown out of the Writers' Union, his works ceased to be published (for 12 years), and he became a "non-person."

1958   Zoshchenko died in Leningrad.

Notes

1. Mikh. Zoshchenko, *Rasskazy*, Gramatu Draugs, Riga, 1927; *Skupoy Rytzar*, Literatura, Riga, 1928.

2. Then, again, maybe it wasn't. Zoshchenko was such a deep and complex person and he lived in such perilous circumstances that very little is known of his intimate beliefs and attitudes. Making positive statements about his intentions is, therefore, rather risky.

Needless to say, after all the bad experiences the Soviet establishment had had with Zoshchenko, it has been extremely chary of anything that has to do with him. Precious little scholarly and biographical material has been published in the USSR about him since 1929. Normally Soviet publishers are great believers in prefaces, introductions, and forewords, and almost every book they publish comes equipped with one or more of these—thorough, comprehensive, and long-winded. Zoshchenko's books, by contrast, are notable for the absence of any commentary whatsoever. Not a word.

3. M. Zoshchenko, *Povesti i rasskazy*, Chekhov Publishing House, New York, 1952

4. M. Zoshchenko, *Izbrannoe*, Khudozhestvennaya Literatura, Leningrad, 1978.

5. Vulgar language, incidentally, has been a perpetual headache for the publishers of Zoshchenko's works. Prissy Soviet censors and editors took every chance to expunge some of Zoshchenko's "son-of-a-bitch's" (*sukin syn*), "bastards" (*svoloch*), and the like, but this robbed the stories of their zest, and so during the more liberal periods some of these were reinstated. Likewise some of Zoshchenko's more outrageous (and hilarious) manhandlings of Russian grammar and syntax were "corrected" only to be later restored—sometimes. Added to this are the constant attempts to make Zoshchenko's message more in line with the official ideology of the moment by such means as deleting sentences or even paragraphs, adding moralistic codas, and inserting words here and there. The result of all this tinkering is that no two editions of Zoshchenko's stories are the same, and there is no way of knowing which changes (if any) were made by Zoshchenko himself. For the purpose of this translation, I relied chiefly on the Chekhov Publishing House edition and the Riga edition.

6. Zoshchenko claimed that he never invented anything, that he only used things he had actually heard. Even if this is true for any particular expression, which I doubt (it is hard to imagine anyone in real life saying "tenorov nynche net"—there are no tenors under the Soviets), the sum total of all these expressions is a uniquely Zoshchenkovian idiom spoken only by Zoshchenko's characters.

A Man Is Not a Flea

The Electrician

I am not going to waste my time arguing with you guys about who is more important in the theater—the actors, the director—or, perhaps, the stage carpenter. I'll give you the facts—facts always speak for themselves.

This whole business happened in Saratov or Simbirsk, in a word, somewhere not too far from Turkestan. In the municipal theater there. They did operas at that municipal theater. Besides the outstanding artistry of the cast, incidentally, this theater engaged the services of an electrician—one Ivan Kuzmich Chaffin.

When, in 1923, they took a group photo of the entire theater company, they stuck this electrician—"mere technical staff"—way over to one side. And in the center, on a chair with a back, they placed the tenor.

The electrician, Ivan Kuzmich Chaffin, said nothing to this outrage at the time, but in his heart he stored up a certain amount of hostility. Particularly since in the picture he came out fuzzy and out of focus.

And now this scenario. Tonight, let's say, *Ruslan and Ludmila* is playing. Music by Glinka. Maestro Katzmann is conducting. And at quarter to curtain time two young ladies, the electrician's friends, turn up looking for him. Maybe he'd invited them beforehand, or they just breezed in on their own—this is not clear. Anyway, these two lady friends of his turn up and, flirting like there is no tomorrow, beg to be seated amidst the theater audience to have a look at the show. The electrician says:

"My goodness, but of course, Mesdames, I'll fix you up with a couple of tickets in a jiffy. Why don't you, for the time being, sit here by my booth."

And, of course, he runs over to see the manager.

The manager says:

"Today happens to be a weekend day. Mobs of people. Every seat is accounted for. Can't help you."

The electrician says:

"Oh, is that so?" he says. "Then I refuse to perform. I refuse, in short, to provide lighting for your production. Go on without me. Then we'll see who is more important around here, and who should be in the center of pictures, and who way off to one side."

Then he goes back to his booth, switches off every damn light in the theater, locks up the booth as tight as a drum, and sits inside with his girlfriends—flirting like there's no tomorrow.

At this juncture, of course, complete discombobulation takes place. The manager rushes about. The crowd yells. The cashier screams, fearing his money might get snitched in the dark. And that bum, the star opera tenor who is in the habit of sitting forever in the center of the picture, reports to the management and says in his tenor voice:

"I refuse to sing tenor in the dark," he says. "If it's dark, I'm leaving. I can't take chances with my voice. Let the son of a bitch electrician sing."

The electrician says:

"So he won't sing. Piss on him. Since the bastard gets the center of the picture, he can sing with one hand and turn the switches on with the other. The nerve of that creep! He thinks just because he's a tenor, you've got to shine light on him all the time. There are no tenors under the Soviets!"

Now, of course, the electrician and the tenor have a go at it.

Suddenly, the manager shows up and says:

"Where are those two dumb broads? On account of them we're witnessing total ruination. I'll seat them somewhere, blast them."

The electrician says:

"Here they are, the dumb broads! Only the ruination is not on account of them, it's on account of me. I'll switch on the lights right away. As a matter of principle, I don't begrudge electrical energy."

He immediately turns the lights on.

"You can proceed," he says.

Then they place his girls in prominent seats and the show starts.

Now, figure out for yourself who is more important in this complex theatrical business.

The Dictaphone

Wow, it's hard to believe what sharp folks those Americans are! How many amazing discoveries they have made, how many great inventions! Steam, Gillette safety razors, the Earth's turning on its axle, all this was discovered and thought up by the Americans and to some extent by the English.

And now behold: once again mankind has reason to rejoice—the Americans have bestowed upon the world a special machine—the dictaphone.

It could be, of course, that this machine was invented somewhat earlier, but we received it only recently.

It was a solemn and unforgettable day when this dandy machine was delivered.

A throng of people gathered to take a look at this marvel.

Our greatly and universally esteemed Konstantin Ivanovich Dimvitkin took the hood off the machine and, filled with awe, wiped the dust off with a rag. And at this moment we could see with our own eyes what great genius it took to invent it. Our gaze was, indeed, confronted with countless screws, rollers, and most intricate thingamabobs. One was even surprised at the thought that a machine which looked so delicate and fragile could function and fulfill its purpose.

Ah, America, America, what a great country it is!

When the machine had been thoroughly examined, our greatly and universally esteemed comrade Dimvitkin, after saying a few things in praise of the Americans, made some introductory remarks about the usefulness of great inventions. After that, practical experiments were undertaken.

"Which one of you," Konstantin Ivanovich said, "wishes to say a few words into this superior apparatus?"

To this, esteemed comrade Basil Tykin came forward. He was a tall fellow, making 27 rubles a week plus overtime.

"Allow me," he said. "Let me test it."

Permission was granted.

He approached the machine with a certain amount of uneasiness, thought for a long time of something to say, couldn't think of anything, and walked away from the machine shrugging his shoulders and feeling sincerely distressed by his illiteracy.

Then another guy walked up. This one wasted little time on thought and yelled into the gaping horn:

"Hey, you, damn fool woman!"

The cover was immediately lifted, the roller taken out and then placed wherever it was supposed to go, and guess what? The roller, exactly and in full, conveyed to all present the words described above.

The delighted members of the audience then took turns elbowing their way to the horn in order to test the machine with their favorite phrase or slogan. The machine obediently recorded everything with complete accuracy.

Now Basil Tykin, who earns 27 rubles plus overtime, came forward once again and proposed that someone from the present company try feeding the horn with some obscene cussing.

The thoroughly esteemed Konstantin Ivanovich Dimvitkin at first categorically forbade swearing into the machine, he even stomped his foot, but then, after some hesitation, he found the idea rather appealing and he sent someone next door to fetch the former Black Sea sailor—a notorious swearer and brawler.

The tar didn't make us wait—he showed up right away.

"Where do I swear?" he said. "Into which opening?"

Well, we showed him, of course. And then he let loose, boy, oh, boy, did he ever let loose! Even the much esteemed Dimvitkin merely threw his hands up in amazement as if to say—get a load of this, it's real hot stuff, even America can't beat that.

After dragging the tar away from the horn by his heels, the roller was switched over. And sure enough, the device again played everything back accurately and unswervingly.

Then everyone walked up to the horn one more time, trying swear words in every cant and dialect. Then they began producing various sounds: They clapped their hands, tap-danced, clicked their tongues—the machine functioned without breaking its stride.

Everyone realized at this point what a clever and outstanding invention it was.

It's too bad, though, that this machine turned out to be somewhat fragile and ill adapted to sharp sounds. So, for example, Konstantin Ivanovich fired a Nagan, not at the horn, of course, but to the side as it were, in order to record on the roller for posterity the sound of a pistol shot—but guess what? It turned out that the machine broke down, it couldn't take it.

So on this account the laurels of American inventors and speculators lost some of their luster and loftiness.

Still, their service for the benefit of humanity has been great and significant.

The Barrel

Well, folks, it sure looks like spring. Then, before you know it, it will be summer. And it sure is nice, comrades, when it is summer. The sun shines real bright. It's hotter'n hell. And you prance around like a big shot with no boots on, just your breeches, and inhale. Cute little birds flutter around somewhere not too far away. Itsy-bitsy gnats pursue their happiness. Beetles bask. Yes, folks, it is nice in the summer.

Nice, of course—very nice, but nothing is perfect.

A couple of years ago we had a cooperative job. That's the turn our lives took—we had to man a counter in a Red Cooperative Store. It was in 1922.

And so, let me tell you, comrades, there's nothing more disgusting as far a cooperative store is concerned than when it's hotter'n hell. Food, you see, goes bad. Now I ask you, does food rot or doesn't it? You bet your life it does. And when it rots, does the cooperative lose money? It sure does.

What's more, maybe they've just then launched a slogan: "No waste in socialist economy." Well, if you don't mind my asking, how do you reconcile these two things, the slogan and summer?

No, my fellow citizens, you should not approach natural phenomena with such utter selfishness as to dance and rejoice when warm weather sets in. You must also, fellow citizens, think of the good of society.

I remember the time, see, when some sauerkraut spoiled in our cooperative; it putrefied, if you'll pardon the homely expression.

And, bad enough, our cooperative suffered a direct financial loss because of this—there were, we soon discovered, overhead expenses. It turned out that we were supposed to have the spoiled goods carted away. How do you like that? They make you throw good money after your own rotted stuff! It just ain't fair.

And the barrel with putrefied sauerkraut was huge. A real monster of a barrel, it must have held eight bushels if it held one. And if you try to figure it out in pounds, it'll come to a zillion. I tell you, it was one big barrel.

And the depressing aroma it gave off—the kiss of death.

Our manager, Ivan Fyodorovich, lost sight of the purpose of his life on account of this rank incense. All he did was walk around and sniff the air.

"Kinda reeks," he would say, "eh, fellows?"

"It doesn't simply reek, Ivan Fyodorovich," we would answer, "it just plain smells."

And, I must admit, the smell was pretty potent. Pedestrians even took pains not to walk on our side of the street. One whiff was enough to knock them off their feet.

Shipping the doggone barrel off to hell would have been the smart thing to do, but our manager, Ivan Fyodorovich, just couldn't make up his mind. Spending the dough gave him a pain, you see. Pay for the cart. Pay for this, pay for that, then pay for something else again. And the stuff had to go clear across town to the boondocks. Nonetheless, in the end the manager said:

"Spending the dough, fellows," he said, "gives me a pain, that's for sure, and it'll cause," he said, "our percentage to deteriorate, but we've got to get rid of this baby. The smell is simply too thick."

Well, we had a guy working there, a salesman, Vaska Verevkin. So he said:

"Listen, comrades, why in blazes should we deport this here barrel, squander money, that life-blood of the people, and also sink our percents? Let's simply roll this lil' ol' barrel out into the yard instead. And then we wait'n see what happens."

So we heaved the barrel out.

When we showed up the next morning, the barrel stood as clean as a whistle. The sauerkraut got stolen during the night.

This development cheered us all up at the cooperative a great deal. The place hummed with work that day like a beehive—that's how much our spirits were lifted. Our manager, good old Ivan Fyodorovich, walked around all day rubbing his hands together.

"Terrific, fellows, just terrific," he kept saying. "Now all the food can go bad if it wants to. We know what to do."

Soon another barrel of sauerkraut went rotten. And a keg of pickles.

That made us mighty happy. We dragged the stuff out into the yard and then opened the gate a crack. For the sake of better visibility. As if to say: "This way, citizens, come'n get it!"

Only this time we got burnt. Not only did they make off with the sauerkraut, but the bastards carried away the barrel too. They also swiped the keg.

From then on we dumped putrefied foodstuff onto old potato sacks.

A Halloween Story

Nobody writes Halloween stories these days. For the good reason that there's nothing particularly hallowed left in our lives.

All the Halloween spookery, the rising dead, and the miracles have receded, as they say, into the realm of legend.

The dead, though, are still with us. About one particular dead man, citizens, I can tell you a story.

This honest-to-God true account was passed on to me by a doctor, a specialist in children's and internal diseases.

This kindly doctor was rather old and his hair was all gray. Whether his hair turned gray as a result of these facts, or did it on its own, is not known. But it was, indeed, gray and his nose was ruddy. The same thing about the nose: it is not known whether it had had outside help in acquiring that hue, or it had come about naturally.

But all this is beside the point.

This doctor, see, was sitting in his office one day, thinking:

"Patients these days," he thought, "are a total loss. Every one of them is out to mooch free medical care at state clinics. Wouldn't dream of seeing a private physician. Let's face it, I'll have to hang up my stethoscope."

Suddenly the doorbell rang.

A middle-aged citizen came in and began complaining about not feeling too well. His heart, he said, kept stopping all the time, and he could just feel it in his bones that he was going to kick the bucket soon after this visit.

The doctor examined the patient—nothing wrong to speak of. The guy was as healthy as a bull, with rosy cheeks and a moustache curling upwards. Everything else in the organism was in its place and no dying of any kind could be perceived.

The doctor wrote him a prescription for anise-sal-ammonia drops, collected 70 kopeks for the visit, shook his head, and, following the canons of his profession, told him to come back again the next day. And that was the end of that.

The next day at the same time a sweet little old lady wearing a black babushka came. She blew her nose every second and cried. She said:

"Not long ago," she said, "my beloved nephew, Vassily

Lollipopov, visited you. Well, you see, he passed away from heart rupture during the night. Could you, in view of this, give him a death certificate?"

The doctor said:

"It's very surprising that he passed away. People," he said, "seldom pass away from anise drops. Nevertheless," he said, "I cannot give you a death certificate—I've got to see the deceased first."

The sweet old lady, God's own little buttercup, said:

"That's absolutely fine with me. Follow me then. It's not far."

The doctor took his bag, put on, mind you, his galoshes, and went out with the sweet old lady.

They got to an apartment building and walked up to the fifth floor. They entered the apartment. It did, indeed, smell of incense there. The deceased was laid out on a table. Candles were burning all around. And the sweet old lady kept grunting pitifully.

A gloomy and disgusted feeling flooded the doctor's heart.

"What an old fart I am," he thought. "How could I be so dead wrong about this patient? Such a hassle for 70 kopeks."

He sat down at the table and quickly wrote out the certificate. He then handed it to the sweet old lady and left as fast as he could, without even saying goodbye.

He walked down the stairs. Got out into the street. And suddenly he remembered—"my goodness, I've forgotten my galoshes!"

"What lousy luck," he thought, "for those same 70 kopeks. Now I've got to trudge up there again."

Up the stairs he went. Entered the apartment. The door, of course, had been left unlocked. And suddenly he saw: sitting on the table lacing up his boot was the deceased Vassily Lollipopov. And as he laced his boot, he argued with the little old lady about something. And the little old lady, God's own little dandelion, was walking around putting out the candles with her finger. She'd spit on her finger and snuff them out.

The doctor was very surprised to see this and wanted to scream out with fright. He thought better of it, however, and, as he was, without his galoshes, rushed out.

He ran all the way home and there fell on the couch, teeth chattering with fear. Then he took some anise-sal-ammonia drops, calmed down, and called the police.

The next day the police cleared up the whole story.

It turned out that the advertising agent Vassily Mitrofanovich Lollipopov had pocketed three thousand rubles of the people's money. With this he had intended to make a clean getaway and begin a splendid new life.

It didn't pan out, however.

The doctor got his galoshes back on the eve of All Saints Day after many tedious requests, forms, and pilgrimages to bureaucratic shrines.

Bathhouse

I've heard, comrades, that bathhouses in America are mighty excellent.

There, for example, a citizen can simply come, shed his clothes into a special box, then wash to his heart's content. He doesn't have a worry in the world, like having his things stolen or lost. He doesn't even bother with claim checks.

Okay, maybe some jittery American will say to the attendant: "Goodbyeski, Mac. Keep an eye on my stuff, will you?"

And that's all.

So this American goes to wash. And when he returns, he gets his underwear back whiter than snow—all washed and ironed. I bet they put brand new cardboard in his shoes to cover up the holes. Even his shorts'll be mended and patched up. That's the life!

Our bathhouses are all right too, but they aren't quite in the same league. Still, they do give you a chance to wash up.

One problem we have is claim checks. Last Saturday I went to the bathhouse—"Can't very well go to America," I said to myself. They gave me two tags, one for the coat and hat, the other for all the rest.

And what's a naked man supposed to do with those tags? Tie them to his beard? All I could see was my belly and my legs, and they don't come with pockets. They were a pain in the neck, those tags.

Okay, so I tied a tag to each leg—that way I wouldn't lose them both at once—and in I went to bathe.

Now the tags kept slapping at my legs. That took all the fun out of walking. Yet I had to walk because I needed a tub. What kind of washing would it be without a tub? A pain in the neck.

So I set out to look for a tub. Soon I found some citizen washing in three tubs. One he was using to stand in, the other one to lather his noggin, and the third one he clenched with his left hand so nobody would swipe it.

I tried to pull that third tub away, thinking, kind of, of taking it for myself, but the citizen wouldn't let go.

"What's the idea," he said, "stealing other people's tubs? I'll give you a tub," he said, "right between the eyes. That'll learn you."

"This isn't tsarist Russia," I said, "to go around smacking

people with tubs. Talk about selfishness," I said. "Other people too would like to wash. Show business," I said, "this isn't."

But he just turned away, bent over, and went on washing.

"It's no use standing here," I thought, "breathing down his neck. Now, just to be ornery," I thought, "he'll take three days to finish washing."

So I went on.

An hour later I saw some geezer slip up: he took his hands off his tub. Maybe he was reaching for his soap, maybe he took to daydreaming, who knows? All I know is, I took that tub for myself.

Okay, now I got myself a tub of my own, but there was no place to sit down. And what kind of washing would it be standing up? A pain in the neck.

Well, anyway. So I stayed standing up on my feet, holding the tub in one hand, and began washing.

In the meantime, people all around me had gone into laundry business. Holy cow! Here was one man washing his pants; there another scrubbing his shorts; a third one was also messing around with something or other. And they all splattered, damn their hides. No sooner would I get some part of me clean—splash! and it was dirty again. And the noise they made with all that rub-a-dub-dubbing! It took all the fun out of washing. Couldn't hear myself think what to soap up next. A pain in the neck, that's what it was.

"They can all go jump in a swamp," I thought. "I'll finish my washing at home."

So I went to the locker room. In exchange for one of the tags, they gave me my clothes. Right away I saw that almost everything was mine—only the pants weren't.

"Citizens," I said, "my pants had a hole right about here. These have one way over there."

The attendant said:

"I ain't paid," he said, "to keep track of holes. Show business," he said, "this ain't."

Okay. I put on these pants and went to get my coat. They wouldn't give it to me—not without a tag. And the tag's on my leg where I left it. Now I had to undress. I took off my pants, looked up and down the leg, found the string, but the paper tag with a number on it was gone. Down the drain.

I offered the attendant my string, but he didn't want it.

"I don't issue nothing for string," he said. "Any citizen," he said, "could show up with a bunch of string. Where'd I get that many coats? Wait around 'til the other customers go home," he said. "Then I'll give you what's left."

I said:

"Oh, come on, buddy, what if some old rag's left? This isn't show business," I said. "I'll describe the article to you," I said. "There's a hole in one pocket," I said, "the other one's long gone. As regards buttons," I said, "the top one is still there," I said, "all the rest are missing in action."

He gave me the coat after all. Without taking the string even.

I got dressed and walked out in the street. Then I remembered— I'd left my soap behind.

Back I went once again. They wouldn't let me in with my coat on.

"Take it off," they said.

I said:

"Fellow citizens, I can't spend my life getting dressed and undressed," I said. "This isn't show business. Why don't you give me at least what the soap cost?"

They wouldn't.

I didn't care any more. I went home without the soap.

Of course, a curious reader may want to know—which bathhouse was this? Where is it? What's the address?

Which bathhouse, you ask? Any old bathhouse. Take your pick.

Lemonade

I'll never kill more than two bottles, no way. My health won't let me. Though I do remember once, when celebrating the day of my ex-saint, I dispatched a whole jug.

But that was in my young and vigorous salad days, when my heart beat full tilt in my chest, and various thoughts crossed my mind.

Now I'm getting old.

The veterinarian's assistant, comrade Birdov, examined me the other day and, you know, he got scared. Began shaking.

"Inside you," he said, "there's total devaluation. There's no way of telling where's the liver and where's the bladder. There's been a lot of wear and tear on you."

I considered beating the assistant up, but my cooler head prevailed.

"Let me first," I thought, "go see a good doctor. Just to make sure."

The doctor didn't find any devaluation.

"Your organs," he said, "are in a fairly neat shape. The bladder," he said, "is quite decent and doesn't leak. As to your heart, it's still in A-one condition, it's even," he said, "bigger than you need. But," he said, "you must stop drinking, otherwise death could routinely occur."

And I, of course, don't want to die. I like to live. I'm still a young fellow. At the beginning of the revolution I had barely turned forty-three. You might say I am in the prime of life and health. I have this large heart in my chest. And, most important, a watertight bladder. With a bladder like that, why shouldn't I go on enjoying life? I really should quit drinking, I thought. So I went and quit.

I laid off the sauce cold turkey. I laid off for one hour, then two. At five o'clock, naturally, I went out to dinner.

I got through the soup. When I started eating boiled meat, I felt like having a drink. In place of spirited beverages, I thought, I'll ask for something milder—mineral water or lemonade. So I summoned the waiter.

"Hey," I said, "which of you bozos served me the soup? Fetch me some lemonade."

They brought me the lemonade, on a fancy-shmantsy tray yet, and in a decanter. I poured some into a jigger.

Well, as I sipped out of that jigger, a strange feeling came over me—by golly, this seems to be vodka. What the hell is going on? I poured the last of it, it was honest to goodness vodka.

"Bring me," I hollered, "more."

Son of a gun, I thought, what luck!

The waiter brought me more.

I tried again. No doubt about it, it was the real McCoy.

Later, when paying the bill, I grilled the waiter.

"I ordered lemonade," I said. "And you, birdbrain, what did you bring me?"

He said:

"We always, like, call it lemonade here. That's a strictly legitimate word. We've been using it since before the revolution... As for natural lemonade, sorry, we don't stock it, there's no demand."

"Bring me," I said, "a last one for the road."

So I never quit. And I wanted to so much. Too bad circumstances prevented me. As the saying goes, life has its own laws. Got to obey them.

An Aristocratic Lady

Friends, I don't like broads who wear hats. If a broad has a hat on, if she wears silk stockings, or totes a pooch in her arms, or else sports a gold tooth, an aristocratic lady like that is, as far as I'm concerned, not a broad at all, but a featureless landscape.

In my day, of course, I did fancy an aristocratic lady. We went for walks and I took her to the theater. This whole thing happened in the theater, as a matter of fact. It was in the theater that she unfurled her ideology to its full extent.

I met her, see, in the courtyard of our building. During a meeting I happened to look up and I saw this dame. Fancy stockings, a gold tooth, the works.

"Where are you from, citizen?" I said. "Which apartment?"

"My apartment," she said, "is number seven."

"It's okay by me," I said. "Enjoy it."

I liked her right off the bat. I started dropping by apartment seven every chance I got. I'd come in my official capacity and ask, like, how's every little thing as regards malfunctioning of the toilet and plumbing? Is everything working?

"Yes," she'd answer, "everything works."

Then she'd wrap herself tighter in her flannel scarf and say not a peep more. She'd just bat her eyes. And flash the tooth in her mouth. I kept coming like this for a month and she got used to me. She'd answer me in greater detail. "Yes, Grigory Ivanovich," she might say, "the plumbing works just fine, thank you."

Well, by and by, things came to a head—we went for walks in the streets. We'd stroll out and she'd insist I offer her my arm. I would, and there I'd be, shuffling along like a penguin. I didn't know what the hell to say to her, and I felt embarrassed in front of people.

Well, one time she said to me:

"Why do you keep," she said, "dragging me around through the streets? It's enough to make my head dizzy. Why don't you," she said, "being a man of the world and a person of importance, take me someplace, to the theater for example?"

"No problem," I said.

It so happened that the very next day the party committee sent over some opera tickets. One ticket I had coming to me; the other one Vassily the pipe fitter contributed to my cause.

I didn't notice it at the time, but they weren't together. My ticket was for a seat downstairs, Vassily's for way up in the gallery.

And so we went. Seated ourselves in the theater. She took my place, I took Vassily's. Couldn't see a damn thing, perched there among the rafters. Except, if I leaned over the railing, I could see her—just barely. After a while I got good and bored, so I made my way down. There I found that intermission was in full swing. And there she was, walking around in the midst of it.

"Hello," I said.

"Hello."

"I wonder," I said, "if the plumbing works here?"

"I don't know," she said, sashaying to the refreshments room. I tagged along. She strolled around the refreshment room and gazed at the counter. There was a platter on the counter. And on that platter was some pastry.

So I, mincing around her like a peacock, like some kind of unreconstructed capitalist, extended an invitation to her:

"If," I said, "you feel like eating one piece of pastry, don't be bashful. I'm buying."

"Merci," she said.

And, wouldn't you know it, she waltzed decadently to the counter and snatch! grabbed a tart with a cream filling and began feeding her face.

And I was flat broke—flatter than an elephant's instep. With luck, I had enough for maybe three of those pastries. While she ate, I gropped worriedly with my hands in my pockets, trying to tell by feel how much money I had.

There wasn't much—as much as a hen has teeth.

After she'd disposed of the cream tart, she grabbed another variety. I gulped, but didn't say anything. I was overcome by some kind of middle-class scruples. A ladies' man, you understand, and no dough.

So I kept strutting around her like a turkey, while she giggled and invited compliments. I said:

"Isn't it time to go back to our seats? Maybe the bell has rung."

And she said:

"No."

Then took a third pastry.

I said:

"Won't it be too much on an empty stomach? You might throw up."

"Oh, no," she said, "we're quite used to it."

Then she took a fourth one.

At this point I blew my top.

"Okay, sister," I said, "put that down!"

That fazed her. She opened her mouth. Her tooth was flashing inside.

But there was no stopping me—I was seeing red. It makes no difference, I thought to myself, she'll never go out with me again.

"Put it back," I said, "damn it!"

She put it back, all right, and I turned to the proprietor:

"How much do I owe you," I said, "for the three consumed pieces of pastry?"

The proprietor played it as cool as a cucumber.

"For the four consumed items," he said, "so much."

"How do you mean four," I said, "when the fourth one is right here on the platter?"

"Nothing doing," he answered. "It may be on the platter, but there is a bite in it and it's been squished with a finger."

"What do you mean, for Pete's sake, 'a bite?' "I said. "It's your ridiculous imagination."

The guy still didn't want to know from nothing. He didn't even bother to answer me, he just waved his hand in front of his kisser.

Well, naturally people gathered around. Experts. Some said there was a bite, others said there wasn't.

I turned my pockets inside out and all kind of junk fell to the floor. Everyone started to laugh except me. I didn't feel like laughing, I was counting money.

I counted up the money—there was exactly enough for four pieces. Son of a gun, I'd argued for nothing. So I paid. Then I turned to the lady:

"Finish it up, citizen," I said, "it's paid for."

But the lady wouldn't budge. She was too embarrassed to finish it.

Now some geezer butted in.

"Let me," he said, "I'll finish it."

And he did, the bastard. Had a little snack on me.

We went back to our posts. We saw the end of the opera. Then we headed home.

And in front of the building the lady said to me:

"That was pretty crummy of you, back there. If you don't have money, you shouldn't go out with ladies."

And I said:
"Money isn't everything, citizen, if you'll pardon my saying so."
That's how we parted.
I don't like aristocratic types.

The Actor

This is an honest to goodness true story. It occurred in Astrakhan. An amateur actor told it to me.

Here's what he told me:

"You're asking me, citizens, if I've ever been an actor. Well, yes, I have. I have performed in a theater. I did come in contact with this form of art. Only it is hogwash. There is nothing peculiarly outstanding about it.

"Of course, if you think about it more deeply, there is much to be said for this form of art.

"Let's say you walk out on the stage, and your public is watching you. And among the public are your friends, relatives on the wife's side of the family, the citizens from your apartment building. You see them winking at you from the front rows, as if to say—'don't get cold feet, Vassya, go for it in spades.' And you flash little signs to them, like, quit worrying, citizens. I'm hip. Wasn't born yesterday.

"But if you reflect more deeply, there's nothing good in this profession. Aggravation mostly.

"There was the time we were putting on the play *Who Is to Blame?* From the pre-revolutionary life. A very powerful play. In one of the acts, you know, robbers rob a merchant in full view of the audience. It comes out very naturalistic. The merchant, you know, yells, kicks for all he's worth. And they rob him. It's a frightful play.

"So we put on this play.

"And just before the show, one of the amateur actors, the one who was supposed to play the merchant, had a few drinks. And because of the heat, the bum got so woozy, we could clearly see he was unable to portray the merchant's role. As soon as he got to the footlights, he began crunching the lightbulbs with his foot.

"The director, Ivan Pavlovich, said to me:

" 'I guess we can't have him out there in the second act. The son of a bitch will squash all the bulbs. Maybe you'll do the part in his place? The public is dumb, won't know the difference.'

"I said:

" 'Citizens,' I said, 'I can't go on stage. Don't even ask. I have,' I said, 'just eaten two watermelons. I can't think straight.'

"But he said:

" 'You've got to help us out, old friend. For one act at least. Maybe the other actor will later pull himself together. Don't wreck our work of enlightenment.'

"They talked me into it after all. Down I came to the footlights.

"And I came on, according to the script, wearing my own jacket and trousers. I only pasted on someone else's beard. And came on. The public, though dumb, recognized me right away.

" 'Hey,' they said, 'that's Vassya up there! Don't get cold feet, go for it in spades...'

"I said:

" 'No time for cold feet, citizens,' I said, 'since we have a crisis back here. The actor,' I said, 'is pretty pickled, and can't appear on stage. He's throwing up.'

"We started the act.

"In the act I play the merchant, you understand. So I yell, and try to kick the robbers away from me. And suddenly I feel one of the amateurs actually reaching into my pocket.

"I pull my jacket tight. Away from the performers.

"I try to fight them off. Bash them right in the kisser. So help me.

" 'Don't come near me,' I say, 'you crumbs. I'm asking you nicely.'

"But they, according to the script, keep after me. They pull out my wallet (ninety rubles) and go for the watch.

"I holler with all my might:

" 'Help, citizens, they are robbing me for real.'

"But this only gives my performance a more realistic effect.

"The dumb public clap their hands in delight. They shout:

" 'Atta boy, Vassya, way to go. Fight them off, ol' buddy. Hit the scoundrels on the head.'

"I yell back:

" 'It doesn't help, friends!'

"And I keep socking them right across the snout.

"I can see one amateur bleeding to death, but the other rascals got all fired up and keep after me.

" 'Friends,' I shout, 'what is this? For what do I have to suffer like this?'

"The director sticks his head out from behind the scenery.

" 'Good man,' he says, 'Vassya. You are carrying your part,' he says, 'marvelously. Keep it up.'

"I can see that yelling doesn't help. Because whatever I yell fits the plot just right.

"So I drop to my knees.

" 'Friends,' I say, 'Director Ivan Pavlovich. I can't take it no more. Drop the curtain.' I say, 'I mean it, they are stealing my last savings from me!'

"At this point many theatrical specialists saw that the words were not according to the play and so they came out from backstage. The prompter, bless him, crawled out of his booth.

" 'It seems, citizens,' he said, 'they have really snitched the wallet from the merchant.'

"They let the curtain down. Brought me water in a pitcher. Gave me to drink.

" 'Friends,' I said, 'Director Ivan Pavlovich. What is this?' I said. 'Following the script, someone pulled my wallet out...'

"Well, they searched the amateur actors. They didn't find the money, though. Only my empty wallet was found backstage where someone had tossed it.

"And so the money was gone. Down the drain.

"Art you say? I've been there! I've performed!"

Adventure Movie

I don't want to badmouth the theater. Still, the movies are my choice. They are a better deal than the theater. You don't have to take your coat off, for instance,—you keep saving quarters that way. Likewise, shaving is optional—nobody can see your face in the dark.

The problem at the movies, though, is getting in. It can be quite tough. You can easily get crushed to death.

As for the rest, it's just dandy. Watching a movie is as easy as pie.

On my spouse's birthday we hied ourselves to the movies to see an adventure film. We bought tickets. Began waiting.

Quite a few people had gathered. And all of them were hanging around the door.

Suddenly the door opened and a young lady said:

"In you go!"

The first few moments there was some pushing. That was because everyone was keen on getting a nice seat.

The folks lunged for the door. And there, at the door, a traffic jam formed.

The people in the back kept pushing, and those in front had no place to go.

And suddenly I got squeezed like a sardine, and swept off to the right.

"Goodness me," I thought, "I hope I don't smash that door."

"Citizens," I yelled, "Take it easy, for God's sake. You might smash the door with a body."

But right then a current formed—there was no way to stop it.

And behind me a military man was shoving me most uncivilizedly. The son of a bitch was literally drilling me in the back.

I kicked that military bum in the shin.

"Quit," I said, "your cheap tricks, citizen."

Suddenly I was lifted up and slammed into the door face first.

"Here we go," I said to myself, "smashing doors with the customers."

I wanted to get away from that door. I tried to ram a passage for myself with my head. They wouldn't let me. Just then I noticed that my pants had gotten hooked on the doorknob. By the pocket.

"Citizens," I yelled, "come on, take it easy. Help! A man is hooked on the door."

The folks shouted back:

"Get unhooked, comrade! The people behind also want to get in."

But how could I get unhooked if I was dragged along unstoppably and in fact could not even move my arm.

"Will you stop," I hollered, "you hellhounds! Don't take my pants off just yet. Give a man a chance to get himself off the knob. The cloth's ripping, for heaven's sake!"

You think they'd listen? They went on stampeding.

"Miss," I said, "for God's sake, you at least look the other way. They are taking me out of my pants against my will, no two ways about it."

But the young lady, herself blue in the face, was already giving the death rattle. And she wasn't in the least interested in looking.

Suddenly, thank goodness, movement became easier.

"Either," I thought, "I got off the knob, or else they took me out of my pants."

Just then a wider passage materialized.

I took a freer breath. Looked around. The pants, I could see, were still there. Only one leg had been split into two halves by the knob, and flapped like a sail as I walked.

"How about that," I thought, "speak of having customers remove articles of clothing."

In this sorry state I went looking for my spouse. Discovered her in the orchestra pit where they'd shoved her. She was sitting there afraid to come out.

Just then, thank goodness, they turned off the lights. They began running the film.

And what kind of film it was I really can't tell you. I spent the whole time trying to pin my pants together.

My wife, bless her, happened to have one pin.

And then some kind-hearted lady took four pins out of her underclothing. I also found a piece of string on the floor. It took me half the show to find it.

So I tied the pants up, pinned them together, and by that time, thank goodness, the adventure ended. We went home.

Happiness

There are times I feel like walking up to a stranger and asking him: "Hey, buddy, how are you doing? Are you pleased with your life? Have you ever known happiness in your life? Come on, take stock of the days gone by."

Ever since they found ulcers in my stomach, I ask people such questions.

Some make wisecracks: "early to bed, early to rise makes me healthy, wealthy and wise." Others lie a lot, like: "I live in luxury, couldn't be better, plenty of double overtime, have a great family."

And only one person answered this question seriously and in detail. That was my dear friend Ivan Fomich Mushin. He was a glazier by trade. A simple soul. Had a beard.

"Happiness, eh?" he asked me. "You bet. Sure I've known happiness."

"Tell me about it," I asked. "Was it a big happiness?"

"Well, big or small, who knows, but I did remember it for the rest of my life."

Ivan Fomich smoked two cigarettes, collected his thoughts, winked at me for some reason, and began his tale.

"This happened, dear comrade, some twenty or twenty-five years ago. I was young and handsome then, my mustache curled upwards, and I was pleased with myself. And I kept waiting, you know, for happiness to come down the pike. In the meantime, the years kept rolling by and nothing special happened. I hardly noticed that I got married, that I got into a fight with my wife's relatives at the wedding, that, soon after, a baby was born. And that one day my wife passed away. And that the baby passed away, too. Everything went along smoothly and quietly. And there was no particular happiness in any of it.

"Then one day, on November 27th, I went to work, and after work—it was almost evening—I stopped in at a tavern and ordered tea.

"So there I was, sipping tea from a saucer. I was thinking that years are rolling by me and no happiness is knocking at my door.

"And just as I thought this, I heard various exclamations. I turned around—there was the owner waving his hand, and a busboy waving his hand, and in front of them stood a soldier of the Tsar's army trying to sit down at a table. The owner, on the other hand, was trying to shove him away from the table and not let him sit down.

"Nope!" the owner shouted. "You soldier people ain't allowed to be seated at tables in taverns. I get to pay a fine for that. You'd better be on your way, my good man."

"But the soldier was drunk and kept trying to sit down. The owner kept shoving. The soldier responded with four-letter words.

"I am," he shouted, "just the same as you. I want to sit down at this table."

"Well, with the patrons' help, the soldier got chucked out. The soldier then grabbed a cobblestone from the pavement and zing! right into the plate glass window. Then he skedaddled.

"And that plate glass measured twelve by nine—worth a mint.

"The owner's arms and legs gave out under him. He crouched down, his head swaying, not daring to look at the window.

"How about that, citizens," he shouted. "That soldier went and ruined me. Today is Saturday, tomorrow's Sunday—two days without the glass. I can't up and find a glazier just like that, and with no glass my customers will be peeved.

"And, indeed, the customers were peeved.

"There's a draft," they said, "from the busted opening. We came to sit in a warm place. Instead—look at that hole."

"Suddenly, I set my saucer on the table, covered the teapot with my hat so it wouldn't get cold, and nonchalantly walked over to the owner.

"My kindly merchant," I said. "I happen to be a glazier."

"Well, he was happy to hear that, he counted the money in the till and asked me:

"How much will the whole shebang cost me? Can you make it out of pieces?"

"Nope," I said, "I'm afraid, my kindly merchant, there's no way to do it with pieces. You need a complete pane—twelve by nine. And the price for that plate glass is 75 rubles and I get to keep what's left of the old one. The price, my kindly merchant, is not competitive and not subject to haggling."

"What? You nuts or something?" said the owner. "Go back to your table and finish your tea. For that amount, I'd be better off plugging up the opening with a comforter."

"And right off he sent his wife home to bring the comforter.

"So the comforter arrived and they stuck it in the hole. But the comforter wouldn't stay put, it kept falling out, or sometimes in, and that caused laughter. Some patrons were offended—it made the place dark, they said, and too ugly to enjoy tea in.

"And one patron, bless him, got up and said:

"I can stare at a comforter at home just as well. What do I need your comforter for?"

"Well, the owner walked over to my table again, begged me to run out and get the glass right away, and gave me the money.

"I didn't bother finishing my tea. I clutched the money in my fist and took off.

"I arrived at the wholesaler's—they were closing. I begged, and I pleaded, and finally they let me in.

"And everything turned out just as I had expected, even better. The twelve-by-nine pane was thirty-five rubles, five for transporting it, forty all told.

"And so I duly replaced the pane.

"I finished drinking my tea, with sugar this time, then ordered fish with sauerkraut and ratatouille to boot. I ate everything and staggered out of the tavern. And in my hand I had thirty rubles—cold cash. If I wanted, I could get plastered, if I wanted... I could do whatever I wanted with it.

"Boy, did I go on a binge then! I didn't sober up for two months. I also bought stuff: a silver ring and warm insoles. Wanted also to buy slacks and a jacket, but ran out of money.

"So, as you can see, my dear comrade, there was a bit of happiness in my life, too. But only once. The rest of my life ran along smoothly, and there was no great happiness in it."

Ivan Fomich fell silent and again, for reasons unknown, winked at me.

I looked at my dear friend with envy. In my life there had never been any such happiness.

Then again, maybe there was, but I just didn't notice it.

A Dog's Nose

Somebody swiped the raccoon coat from Jeremy Babkin, the merchant.

The merchant Jeremy Babkin let out a howl. He was upset, you see, about losing that coat.

"It was," he said, "a mighty fine coat, citizens. It's a shame to lose it. I'll spare no expense, but I'll find the criminal. I'll fix his wagon."

And so Jeremy Babkin summoned a law-enforcing bloodhound. A fellow wearing a cap and gaiters showed up, and with him was the dog. Not just any old dog, but a great big hound, brown, with a pointy snout, and unfriendly.

The fellow shoved the dog at the footprints by the door, said "pss," and stepped back. The dog sniffed the air, ran an eye over the crowd (people had, of course, gathered around), and suddenly approached Grandma Thelma from apartment five and began smelling the hem of her skirt.

Granny tried to hide behind other people. The dog grabbed the skirt. Granny tried to get away, the dog followed. It held Granny by the skirt and wouldn't let go.

Granny dropped to her knees in front of the agent.

"Yes," she said, "you got me. I won't deny it. And," she said, "the five buckets of batter, that's right. And the camera, that, too, is, indeed, true. Everything," she said, "is in the bathroom. Take me to the police station."

Well, the folks, of course, gasped.

"And the fur coat?" they asked.

"About the coat," she said, "I don't have the foggiest and know nothing. But all the rest, that's so. Lock me up, throw away the key."

Well, they took Granny away.

Again the agent took his great dog, again he shoved its nose at the footprints, said "pss," and stepped back.

The hound cast the eye, sniffed the thin air, and suddenly walked up to the comrade building manager.

The building manager turned pale and fell supine to the ground.

"Tie my hands behind my back," he said, "good people, honest citizens. I," he said, "collected money for water, and that money I spent on my own whims and pleasures."

Well, the tenants, of course, set about the building manager and began tying his hands behind his back. And the mighty hound, meantime, walked up to the citizen from apartment seven. Tugged at his pants.

The citizen turned pale, knelt before the people.

"Guilty," he said, "guilty. It is a fact," he said, "that I fudged my age in my work papers. I should be serving," he said, "young bull that I am, in the army defending my fatherland, and instead here I am, living in apartment seven, availing myself of electrical energy and other communal services. Throw the book at me!"

The folks became disconcerted.

"What kind of amazing dog is this?" they thought.

And the merchant Jeremy Babkin blinked his eyes, looked around, pulled out some money and offered it to the agent.

"Get that awful dog of yours," he said, "the dickens out of here. I don't want," he said, "to bitch about the raccoon coat any longer. The hell with it..."

But the awful dog was already on the spot, right in front of the merchant, wagging its tail.

The disconcerted merchant Jeremy Babkin tried to sidle off, but the dog stuck to him. Came up to him and began sniffing at his galoshes.

The merchant bleated a couple of times, then turned pale.

"All right," he said, "if this is the way it is, I guess God sees the truth. I am the one," he said, "who's a son of a bastard and a con artist. Yonder coat, friends," he said, "isn't mine at all. That coat," he said, "I hooked from my brother. I rue and shed tears of repentance!"

The people rushed off headlong in all directions. The frightful hound had no time to sniff the air—just grabbed two or three guys, whoever was within reach, and held them.

They confessed, all right. One had blown public money at cards, the other one had bonked his spouse with a flat-iron, and the third one told things too embarrassing for me to repeat.

And now all the folks were gone. The yard was empty. Only the dog and the agent were left.

And thereupon the dog suddenly walked up to the agent and wagged its tail. The agent turned pale, dropped to his knees before the dog.

"Go ahead," he said, "bite me, comrade dog. I get thirty rubles for your canine rations," he said," but I keep twenty for myself..."

What happened next is not known. I got myself out of harm's way as fast as I could.

A Lamentable Incident

Say what you want, friends, but I have a lot of sympathy for Nikolay Ivanovich.

The dear fellow shelled out all of six bits and saw nothing particularly outstanding for his money.

All because he is such a gentle and unassertive guy, that's the thing. Somebody else in his place might have torn the whole movie house down brick by brick and chucked all the patrons out. After all, you don't find six bits lying on the sidewalk every day. Got to understand.

Last Saturday, see, our good old Nikolay Ivanovich tossed off a few. On account it was payday.

And this man had a fine understanding of the new socialist morality. Some other guy under the influence might have gone all to pieces and made a major nuisance of himself, while Nikolay Ivanovich simply took a quiet and decent stroll along the boulevard. Sang some song or other. Suddenly he saw he was in front of a movie theater.

"Why don't I," he thought, "go see a movie. Might as well. I am, after all, a somewhat educated man, semi-egghead, why should I waste my time bumping into pedestrians while pounding the sidewalks in a drunken state? Why don't I look at a flick in a drunken state? I've never seen anything like that before."

So he bought himself a ticket with his hard-earned cash. And sat in the front row. There he was, sitting in the front row in a quiet and decent manner watching the picture.

He had only seen a couple of the opening credits, perhaps, when he suddenly had to go to Barftown. For it was kind of warm in the movie, see, people were breathing, and darkness affects the psyche that way.

So there he was, our good Nikolay Ivanovich, taking a trip to Barftown, in a quiet and decent manner. He wasn't bothering anyone, he wasn't grabbing for the screen, he wasn't unscrewing the lightbulbs, he just sat there traveling quietly to Barftown.

Suddenly the patrons began to express their displeasure, on account, that is, of Barftown.

"You could, comrade," they said, "take a walk down to the

foyer for this purpose. Here you provide distraction to other patrons trying to see the canned drama by giving them other ideas.''

Nikolay Ivanovich, a somewhat educated man with a fine understanding of the new socialist morality, did not, of course, waste his time arguing and getting upset. He simply got up and quietly left.

"It's no use," he thought, "getting involved with sober people. They can give you a whole lot of trouble."

He went to the exit. Spoke to the box-office person.

"Just now, little lady," he said, "a ticket was purchased from you. Refund the money back to me, please. 'Cause I can't look at the picture, I get the heaves in the dark."

The cashier said:

"We cannot give money back—if you get the heaves, go quietly to bed."

There ensued an uproar and an exchange of abuse. Somebody else in Nikolay Ivanovich's place would have dragged the cashier out of the box by her hair and gotten his hard-earned cash back. But Nikolay Ivanovich is a quiet and civilized man, and all he did was, perhaps, shove the cashier once.

"Get it through your head," he said, "you germ, I haven't looked at your flick. Give me," he said, "my hard-earned cash back."

And he did it all in such a quiet and decent manner, no ruckus or anything—the man just simply wanted his very own money returned.

Now the manager showed up.

"We," he said, "don't return no money back; if," he said, "you paid up, kindly go in and see the rest of the picture."

Someone else in Nikolay Ivanovich's place would have given the manager the finger and gone off for a stroll. But Nikolay Ivanovich was upset about his money, so he began heatedly to reason with the manager and took a return trip to Barftown.

Now, of course, they grabbed Nikolay Ivanovich like a dog, and dragged him off to the police station. They kept him there 'til morning. And in the morning they fined him three smackers and let him go.

I am now very sorry for Nikolay Ivanovich. I don't know, it was such a lamentable incident: the man didn't get to see any of the flick, all he did was hold onto the ticket for a little while, and, mind you, for that minor pleasure had to fork over thirty bits. Thirty bits for what, I ask you?

Thieves

Let me tell you, citizens, there are an awful lot of thieves around these days.

You simply can't find a man who hasn't been robbed.

I myself was relieved of my suitcase just recently. Do you know where Zhmerinki is? Well, it happened just before our train got there.

What can be done, I wonder, about this social affliction? Maybe we could tear thieves' hands off?

I've heard, you see, that in the old days in Finland they used to cut off thieves' hands. Should they catch one of their Finnish comrades stealing, for instance, chop-chop, and off goes the son of a bitch, handless. Damn trustworthy people they've got out there as a result. They tell me they don't even lock their doors. And if, for instance, a Finn drops his wallet in the street, nobody'll take the wallet either. They'll put it somewhere well in sight and let it sit there 'til hell freezes over... My goodness, what fools!

Yeah, but I bet you they'll remove the money from the wallet first. No way they won't. You can hack people's heads clean off, not just hands, and still, I'm sure, it won't do a bit of good. With money, though, it's easy come, easy go. You'd get your wallet back, and that's nothing to sneeze at.

As I was saying, just before we got to Zhmerinki they swiped my suitcase—gone without a trace. Gone with all the innards. They didn't even leave the handle. I had a sponge in the suitcase, worth a nickel maybe, they took that too. What in hell do the dumb bastards need that sponge for? They'll throw it away, the bums, that's for sure. Never mind. They took it just the same.

The thing is, mind you, that night in the train some fellow came over and sat next to me.

"Do me a favor," he said, "be extra careful traveling here. The thieves around here," he said, "are something else. Passengers get picked cleaner than hound's teeth."

"That," I said, "doesn't scare me none. I always lie down," I said, "with my ear to the suitcase. I'll hear."

He said:

"The ear has nothing to do with it. These are clever operators," he said, "they pull boots off people's feet. Never mind the ear."

"My boots, on the other hand," I said, "are tight. They'd never get them off."

"Well, then," he said, "go to hell. I thought I'd warn you. And you do as you please."

That's where matters stood when I dozed off.

Suddenly, just before Zhmerinki, somebody in the dark gave my foot this vicious yank. Honest to God, he nearly ripped my leg off... I jumped up like a startled rabbit and pow! whacked the thief one on the shoulder. Lickety-split he skedaddled off. I tumbled down from my upper berth in pursuit. But I couldn't run.

'Cause my boot, see, was half off, with my foot stuck in the middle.

I started hollering. Stirred up everyone in the car.

"What is it?" they asked.

"My boots, citizens," I said. "They nearly heisted my boots."

I began pulling my boot on when I saw it—my suitcase was gone.

I started hollering all over again. I searched all the passengers—no suitcase.

At the next large station I went to the cops to report the theft.

They were quite sympathetic, wrote it all down.

I said:

"If you catch him, tear his goddamn hands right off."

They laughed.

"O.K.," they said, "will do. Put that pencil back, though."

And, indeed, I simply don't know how it happened, but I had in fact picked up their blue ink pencil from the desk and stuck it in my pocket.

A detective said:

"Over a short period of time, passengers have stolen," he said, "from this place—a police station, damn it, all our desk inventory. Some son of a bitch even carried off the inkwell—ink and all."

I apologized about the pencil and walked out.

"On second thought, if we start cutting off hands around here," I reflected, "we'll have one hell of a lot of disabled people running about. A man can't be too careful."

The Charms of Civilization

I have always been in sympathy with convictions from the center.

Even, if you recall, when during military communism they introduced the New Economic Policy, I didn't protest. If the Party says N.E.P., I say N.E.P. The party knows best.

But, now that I think of it it, when the N.E.P. was introduced, there was an awful sinking feeling in the pit of my stomach. I guess deep down inside I had a premonition that there would be some sharp changes.

And indeed, under military communism things were mighty free and easy with respect to culture and civilization. In the theater, say, you were free not to undress—you could sit the way you came. That was quite an achievement.

And the problem of civilization is a bitch of a problem. Take that same question of undressing in the theater. Of course, there's no arguing, the audience stands to better advantage without overcoats—looks more handsome and more elegant. But things that are good in the bourgeois countries have a way of turning sour in our land.

Comrade Loktev and his ladyfriend Nyusha Koshelkov met me recently in the street. I was taking a walk, or, perhaps, was on my way to wet my tonsils, I don't remember which.

They met me and came on strong:

"Your tonsils, Vassily Mitrofanych," they said, "are not going to run away. Your tonsils are always with you, and you can always wet them. Why don't you come to the theater with us today. The show is 'The Heater.' "

And so, to make a long story short, they talked me into going to the theater with them to soak up some culture.

So, sure enough, we arrived at the theater. And, sure enough, bought our tickets. Then we started up the stairs. Suddenly they hailed us back. They told us to take our coats off.

"Hey, youse," they said, "off with them coats."

Loktev and his lady, of course, instantly took their overcoats off. And I, of course, stood there brooding. That night I had the overcoat on right over my nightshirt. No jacket. And I could sense, friends, that stripping the coat off might be somewhat awkward. "An honest to goodness indecent exposure," I thought to myself, "is bound to occur." It wasn't that my shirt was dirty. No, the shirt wasn't all that dirty. But it sure wasn't a fine shirt. What do you want for God's sake—it was a nightshirt. It had this great big brass button at the neck, the one I'd salvaged off a military tunic. "Plumb indecent," I thought, "going to the foyer with such an oversized button as that." So I said to my friends:

"Honestly, comrades," I said, "I simply don't know what to do. I'm not dressed too well today. Taking my overcoat off might be somewhat awkward. The suspenders, you know, and also my shirt is, well, not a fine shirt."

Comrade Loktev said:

"Well, show us."

I unbuttoned the coat. Showed them.

"Yeah," he said, "a sight. You weren't kidding..."

The lady, of course, also looked and said:

"I'd better," she said, "go home. I can't have escorts walking next to me in nothing but shirts. It's a good thing you got your trousers and your underwear on in the right order. You should be ashamed of yourself patronizing theaters in such an abstract get-up as this."

I said:

"I didn't know I was going to patronize theaters, you cluck. Maybe I seldom wear jackets. Maybe I don't want to wear them out—did you think of that?"

We started wondering what to do. Loktev, the lout, said:

"Tell you what. I'll presently, Vassily Mitrofanovich," he said, "give you my vest. You put my vest on and pretend you'd be much too hot wearing a jacket all the time."

He unbuttoned his jacket and began feeling and groping inside it.

"Oh my goodness," he said, "I myself am not provided with a vest today. Let me better give you my necktie—it'll make you look somewhat more decent. Tie it around your neck and pretend you're too hot all the time."

The lady said:

"Honest to God," she said, "I'd better go home. There, at least, I could relax. Here I have one escort almost in his underwear, and another with a necktie instead of a jacket. Let Vassily Mitrofanovich ask to go in in his overcoat."

We asked, and we begged, we showed our trade union cards,

they still wouldn't let us in.

"It ain't your 1919," they said, "to sit around in overcoats."

"Well," I said, "looks like I've got to mosey on home, that's all there's to it."

But when I remembered that I'd paid cash to get in, I couldn't leave. My legs refused to carry me to the door.

Loktev, the lout, said:

"Tell you what. Take your suspenders off," he said, "let the lady carry them instead of a purse. And you march in as you are; pretend that this is a sports shirt 'Apache', and that you'd simply be much too hot wearing a jacket all the time."

The lady said:

"Say what you want, I'm not carrying any suspenders. I don't go to the theater," she said, "to carry articles of men's apparel in my hands. Let Vassily Mitrofanovich carry them himself, or else let him stick them in his pocket."

I stripped off my coat. And stood there like a son of a bitch in that shirt of mine.

And it was pretty damn cold. I tell you, I was shivering and my teeth were chattering. And there were people all around—watching.

The lady replied:

"Will you hurry up already with the unbuttoning, you klutz! Don't you see all these people walking around? Gee, honest to God, I ought to go home right now!"

But I couldn't unbutton in a hurry. I was cold. My fingers, see, refused to obey me when it came to quick unbuttoning. I had to do warm-up exercises with my fingers.

Eventually we straightened everything up and went to our seats.

The first act went by just fine. Except that I was cold. Had to do calisthenics during the whole act.

Suddenly in the intermission the folks sitting behind me kicked up a fuss. They called the management. To explain about me.

"The ladies," they said, "find it repulsive to look at nightshirts. It shocks them. Besides," they said, "he won't stay still for a second—keeps wriggling like a son of bitch."

I said:

"I wriggle because I'm cold. You should try sitting here in nothing but a shirt. Do you think, friends, I'm enjoying this? But what can I do?"

So they dragged me, of course, over to the office. Wrote everything down.

Then they let me go.

And now they tell me I'll have to pay a three ruble fine in court.

That's really disgusting. You can never guess where trouble will strike next...

Frazzled Nerves

A fight recently occurred in our communal apartment. Actually, not simply a fight, but a full-fledged combat. At the corner of Birch and Linden.

Everyone, of course, fought wholeheartedly. Peg-leg Gavrilych nearly had his one and only block knocked off.

The main reason for it—people's nerves these days are just too frazzled. People get upset over the tiniest trifles. They lose their cool. And that makes them fight crudely, mindlessly, as if blindfolded.

I've been told, of course, that people's nerves get rattled every time there's a civil war. This may well be so, but this bit of sociology isn't going to make Peg-leg Gavrilych's noggin heal up any faster.

Anyway, as I was saying, that evening at nine, one of our tenants, Maria Vassilevna Snipov, came to the kitchen and started to light the kerosene burner. She always, you see, lights the burner around this time. She drinks tea and soaks her arthritic joints.

So she came to the kitchen. She set the kerosene burner in front of her, and tried to light it. But the burner, damn it to hell, wouldn't light.

She thought:

"Why won't the dumb thing light up? Maybe it's full of soot, damn it to hell."

And so she picked up a pipe cleaner in her left hand intending to clean out the burner.

There she was, holding the pipe cleaner in her left hand, ready to start cleaning out the burner, when another tenant, Daria Petrovna Nagin, the owner of the pipe cleaner, looked at the misappropriated article and replied:

"By the way, Maria Vassilevna dear, would you put that pipe cleaner right back where you found it, if you don't mind?"

Snipov, of course, flared up at these words and replied:

"You can stick your pipe cleaner," she replied, "up your nose, Daria Petrovna. I wouldn't touch your pipe cleaner with a ten-foot pole," she said, "let alone take it in my hand."

Now, of course, it was Daria Petrovna's turn to flare up at these words.

A neighborly conversation started up. The apartment filled up with noise, clatter, and bang.

The husband, Ivan Stepanovich Nagin, the co-owner of the pipe cleaner, showed up to see what the noise was all about. He was a sturdy fellow, you know, pot-bellied even, but his nerves too were frazzled.

Anyway, he showed up and said:

"I work," he said, "like a goddamn elephant in a cooperative store for thirty-two rubles and change," he said, "smiling at the customers while I weigh kielbasa for them, and out of that, with my hard-earned kopecks, I buy myself pipe cleaners. And there's no way, I want you to know," he said, "that I'd allow unauthorized personnel to take advantage of those pipe cleaners."

Now there was more noise and discussion regarding the pipe cleaner. All the tenants, of course, gathered in the kitchen. Busybodies, you understand. Peg-leg Gavrilych also gathered there.

"What's all this noise," he said, "and no fight?"

Right after these words the fight materialized. All hell broke loose.

And the kitchen, see, was kind of narrow. Not at all handy to fight in. It was crowded. Pots and kerosene burners all over the place. And, mind you, twelve people had jammed in there. You could hardly move. Suppose, for example, you wanted to smash some guy in the kisser; instead you walloped three others. And, of course, you kept bumping into things, falling down. Never mind the gimpy Gavrilych, you couldn't have stayed on your feet even if you had three legs.

But Peg-leg Gavrilych, the peppery cuss, got right into the thick of it. Ivan Stepanych, the pipe-cleaner owner, yelled out to him:

"Get out of harm's way, Gavrilych, or else they'll break your last leg off."

Gavrilych said:

"Perish the leg," he said. "I can't quit now," he said. "They've just knocked all of my dander up."

Which was true. Somebody had just socked him smack-dab in the puss. So he didn't go away, kept on charging. That was the moment someone hit the handicapped guy right on the noodle with a pot.

The Peg-leg—flop!—fell to the floor. He lay there, all the joy gone out of his life. That's when some pest went to call the police.

A cop showed up and shouted:

"Order your coffins in a hurry, you devils, because I'm about to start shooting."

Only after these fateful words did the folks simmer down a bit. They rushed to their rooms.

"Son of a gun, esteemed citizens," they thought, "what was all this fighting over?"

All the folks had rushed to their rooms, only Peg-leg Gavrilych was still around. He was still lying on the floor, feeling no joy. And blood was oozing from his noggin.

Two weeks after these facts the trial was held.

It turned out that the people's judge also had frazzled nerves— he fixed our wagon, but good.

Westinghouse Brake

The main point is, Volodka Bokov was a mite stewed. Otherwise, of course, he would never have committed such a crime. He was plastered.

If you want to know, just before boarding the train Volodka Bokov had a pint of Stolichnaya and chased it down with beer. As for eating, do you know what he had? Only a bit of pork saussage. You call that food? No wonder he was bombed. A dynamite mixture like that will make your head whirl, spawn all kinds of ideas in your bosom, and make you ham it up for the gallery.

So Volodka boarded the train and began to assert himself a trifle. He is the kind of guy, you understand, who can do anything. Even the People's Court will stand up for him if need be. Because, he wanted everyone to know, his origins were simply too outstanding. For one, his very own granddad was a cowherd. For another, his ever-loving mother was nothing but a simple peasant...

Well, Volodka just kept on wagging his tongue—that's the kind of mood he was in, he felt like bragging. But at this point, in the seat across from Volodka, a citizen manifested himself. He had cotton in his ear and was dressed neatly, even nattily. So he said:

"You just keep up," he said, "that malarkey of yours, and they'll run you in at the next whistle stop."

Volodka said:

"Don't you touch my social awareness. There ain't no way they can run me in 'cause of my powerful background. I'll do anything you like and get away with it."

Well, that's the frame of mind he was in. What do you want— he was drunk.

The people, meanwhile, began voicing their objections on this subject. And the most obnoxious ones started baiting him. One of them, a fellow wearing a blue cap who had a particularly rotten mind, said:

"Why don't you, good buddy," he said, "give this here window a knock so it busts to smithereens," he said, "while we watch to see if they run you in, or let you go scot-free. Or wait," he said, "even better, never mind the window, instead stop the train by means of this handle... It's the brake..."

Volodka said:

"What handle? Which? Where?" he said. "Talk sense, you parasite."

The guy in the blue cap answered:

"This one, here. It's a Westinghouse brake. Yank it from the left, like so."

The people around, including the citizen with cotton in his ear, tried, of course, to stop the instigator: "You should be ashamed of yourself, putting sober ideas into a stewed head."

But Volodka Bokov stood up and yanked the handle as hard as he could.

Suddenly there was total silence among the passengers. Everyone shut up at once. All you could hear was the train doing clickety-click. Nothing else.

The guy in the blue cap gulped.

"How about that," he said, "the pest went and did it..."

Now the folks jumped to their feet. The guy in the blue cap tried to sneak out of harm's way. The other passengers wouldn't let him.

The man with ear-cotton said:

"This is hooliganism. The train will presently stop. The rolling stock will suffer wear and tear. Besides, there'll be a delay."

Volodka Bokov was a bit scared himself.

"Hold the guy with the blue cap," he said. "Let's both go to jail. He made me do it."

The train, meanwhile, showed no obvious signs of stopping.

The folks said:

"A train can't stop on a dime. Even though this is a milk run train, it's still supposed to have inertia, seventy-five yards of it. On wet rails, even more."

The train, meanwhile, kept rolling merrily along.

A mile went by, no stopping is observed.

The person with cotton in his ear said:

"Looks like the brake is, you know... phffft..."

Volodka said:

"What did I tell you? Nobody'll do nothing to me, not a damn thing. Nyah-nyah."

And he sat down. At the next stop he stepped out for a breath of air, freshened up, and arrived home as sober as a judge.

Shortage

The other day, citizens, I saw a cart full of bricks going down the road. So help me!

You know, that set my heart fluttering with joy. It means we are building up. They weren't carrying bricks for nothing. A little old house is going up somewhere. It has started—knock on wood!

In, maybe, twenty years or even less, every citizen, I bet you, will have an entire room to himself. And if the population doesn't increase too rapidly and everyone is allowed to have an abortion, then two even. Maybe even three per head. Plus a bath.

That will be the life, eh, citizens! In one room you can, say, sleep, in another you can entertain company, and do something else yet in the third one... Who knows! If life gets to be so roomy, it will be easy to find things to do.

For the time being, though, things are difficult in the matter of square footage. It is kind of tight because of the housing shortage.

You see, friends, I lived in Moscow. I have just recently returned from there. I had a taste of that shortage myself.

I arrived, see, in Moscow. Walked through the streets with my things. And, I tell you, no dice. Not only I had no place to stay, I had nowhere to leave my things.

Two weeks I walked in the streets with my things. I grew a beard and lost my things one by one. And so, unencumbered with luggage, I continued walking—looking for a place to stay.

Finally in an apartment building I met a man coming down the stairs.

"For thirty rubles," he said, "I can put you up in our bathroom. The apartment," he said, "is fit for a lord... Three toilets... A bathroom... In that bathroom you can live happily ever after. True, there are no windows, but, on the other hand, there is a door. And water is close at hand. You can," he said, "run the tub full of water and dive in it all day long if you want to."

I said: "I, my dear comrade, am not a fish. I have no great necessity to dive," I said. "I'd just as soon," I said, "live on dry land. Knock down the price some," I said, "on account of wetness."

He said:

"I can't, comrade. I'd love to, but I can't. It does not depend entirely on me. It's a communal apartment. And we have worked out a firm price for the bathroom."

"Well," I said, "what can I do? O.K. Gouge," I said, "thirty rubles off me, only," I said, "let me in in a hurry. I've been tramping the sidewalks for three weeks. I am afraid I might get tired soon."

All right. They let me in. I started living there.

And the bathroom was, indeed, fit for a lord. Whichever way you went, you ran into the bathtub, water-heater, or faucets. But, by the way, there was no place to sit. Except, perhaps, on the edge of the bathtub, but it was all too easy to slide straight down into the marble bathtub.

So I made a cover out of boards, and went on living.

In a month, by the way, I got married.

I happened to pick a very young, good-natured spouse. She didn't have a room.

I thought she'd turn me down on account of the bathroom, and I'd never know family bliss and comfort, but she didn't mind, she didn't turn me down. She only frowned a little and answered:

"Well," she said, "nice folks live in bathrooms too. If nothing else, we can make a partition. Here," she said, "would be, say, the boudoir, and here the dining room..."

"It would be possible, citizen, to make a partition, but the damned tenants won't allow it. Even as it is, they keep saying: 'no alterations.' "

Well, áll right. So we went on living as is.

In less than a year my spouse and I had a little baby.

We named him Volodka and went on living. We bathed him right there, in the bathtub, and life went on.

And it was rather neat. The kid had a bath every day and never ever caught a cold.

There was only one inconvenience—in the evening all the communal tenants barged into the bathroom to wash.

During that time my family and I had to retreat to the hallway.

Sure I begged the tenants:

"Citizens," I said, "take baths Saturdays. It makes no sense for you to bathe every day. When am I to live? Put yourselves in my place."

And there were thirty-two of those bums. All of them with bad tempers. They threatened to punch me in the nose if I made any trouble.

Well, what could you do? There was nothing to do. We went on living as is.

In a while my wife's mom arrived in our bathroom from the provinces. Settled behind the water-heater.

"I have been dreaming for a long time," she said, "about rocking a grandson. You can't," she said, "refuse me this entertainment."

I said:

"Nobody's refusing you. Go to it, mom, rock to your heart's content. See if I care. You can run the bathtub full of water and dive in it with your grandson."

And I said to my wife:

"Perhaps, citizen, more of your relatives will arrive, so tell me right away, don't keep me in suspense."

She said: "Not really, except, possibly, my kid brother for Christmas vacation..."

Without waiting for the kid brother I left Moscow. Now I am sending money to my family by mail.

Of Cats and Men

We have this huge brick corner stove in our apartment. It's in terrible shape. The whole family's forever going crazy in the head from monoxide poisoning. And the damn housing commission refuses to authorize repairs. Trying to save money. To cover the next embezzlement.

The other day they examined that stove of ours. They looked at dampers and things. Plunged their heads into the inside.

"Nope," they said, "you can live with it."

"Comrades," I said, "you should be somewhat ashamed to utter words like that—'You can live with it.' We're forever getting monoxided out of our minds as a result of your stove. The other day even the cat got sick. It threw up the other day over there, by the pail. And you say 'You can live with it.' "

The damn housing commission said:

"In that case," it said, "let's set up an experiment and see if your stove monoxides. If, right after we light it, we get monoxided, you're in luck—we'll rebuild it. If we don't—sorry for wasting your firewood."

So we lit the stove. We took our places around it.

And we sit. And sniff.

There, by the damper, sat the chairman. Over here, the secretary, Briboedov. And over there, on my bed, the treasurer.

Soon, of course, fumes began wafting through the room.

The chairman sniffed and said:

"Nope. Can't detect a thing. Only warm emanations spreading around, that's all."

The treasurer, that toad, said:

"An altogether excellent atmosphere. You can sniff it to your heart's content. No loss of efficiency in the head. In my apartment," he said, "the atmosphere stinks much worse than this and still," he said, "I don't go around bellyaching about it. These emanations are well within normal parameters."

I said:

"Come now. What do you mean 'normal'? Look at the gases streaming out."

The chairman said:

"Call in the cat. If the cat sits still, that means there's not a damn thing wrong with your air. An animal is always objective in such matters. Unlike a human. You can put your trust in animals."

The cat came. Settled on the bed. And sat there quietly. No wonder it sat quietly, of course, it was by now somewhat used to the gas.

"Nope," said the chairman. "We're sorry."

Suddenly the treasurer started toppling over on the bed and said:

"I've just remembered some urgent business I have to take care of."

With this, he beelined it to the window and there breathed from a crack.

He stood there green all over and swayed on his feet.

The chairman said:

"We all have to go soon."

I dragged him away from the window.

"That's no way," I said, "to establish an expert opinion."

He said:

"As you wish. I can move away. Your air agrees with me just fine. Natural air, wholesome to your health. I can't rebuild the stove. It's a perfectly normal stove."

Half an hour later, when they were laying this chairman on a stretcher and subsequently shoving the stretcher into the ambulance, I again got to have a talk with him.

I said:

"Well, what do you say?"

"Afraid not," he said, "no repair. You can live with it."

And that was that. They never fixed it.

Well, what can you do? I'm getting used to it. A man is not a flea—he can get used to anything.

Insufficient Packaging

Nowadays people don't take bribes. That was before. Then you couldn't take a step without giving or taking a bribe.

But presently people's character has changed considerably toward the better.

People indeed don't take bribes.

The other day we were at a freight station shipping off some goods.

Our aunt had died from the flu and in her last will and testament she instructed us to send all kinds of bedsheets and other petty-bourgeois stuff to the provinces to some kin on our wife's side of the family.

So here we are at the station watching the following tableau in the spirit of Raphael.

There is the booth where they take shipments. A line, of course. A decimal metric scale. A weighmaster by the scale. The weighmaster, an outstandingly worthy official, calls out the figures, writes things down, shifts weights on the scales, puts stickers on, and provides explanations.

All you hear is his pleasant voice:

"Forty. One-twenty. Fifty. Take it off. Here, grab this. Move back. Don't dump it here, dummy, put it over on that side."

What a lovely picture of work and efficiency.

Suddenly we notice that the weighmaster, though doing beautiful work, is a stickler for regulations. He is ever so concerned about the interest of the citizen and the state. Well, not everyone, but every second or third citizen gets turned away—the weighmaster won't accept his freight. If the packaging is to the least extent flimsy, he won't take it. Although it's obvious that he is sympathetic.

The folks with weak packaging, they, of course, moan and agonize.

The weighmaster tells them:

"Instead of agonizing, get your packaging beefed up. There's a guy with nails hanging around. Let him strengthen it. Let him drive in a couple of nails and tighten it with wire. Then come out of turn—I'll take it."

This is, in fact, true: behind the booth stands a fellow. In his hands are nails and a hammer. He works with sweat on his brow and reinforces flimsy packaging for all who so desire. And the people who had been turned down look at him prayerfully and offer him their friendship and money for you know what.

And now it is the turn of some citizen. He is blondish, wears glasses. He is not an egghead, he is near-sighted. He, I guess, has trachoma in his eyes. And he has put the glasses on so that he won't be seen too well. Or, perhaps, he works at the optical factory, and there they give out glasses for free.

So he plops his six crates on the metric decimal scale.

The weighmaster examines his six crates and says: "Weak packaging. It won't do. Take 'em away."

The guy in glasses, hearing these words, becomes totally depressed. But before becoming depressed, he lights into the weighmaster so ferociously that they almost come to swapping knuckle sandwiches. The guy in glasses yells:

"What are you doing to me, you skunk! I," he says, "am not sending my own crates. I'm sending," he says, "government crates from the optical factory. What am I to do with these crates? Where am I going to find a cart? Where am I going to get a hundred rubles to take them back? Answer me, you skunk, before I make hamburger out of you."

The weighmaster answers: "How should I know?" and waves him away with his hand.

The guy with glasses, on account of his nearsightedness and because of fog on his lenses, takes this gesture to mean something else. He flushes, remembers something he had forgotten long ago, digs in his pockets and pulls out about eight rubles, all in one-ruble notes. And he wants to give them to the weighmaster.

The weighmaster turns crimson at the sight of this money.

He shouts: "How am I to understand this? Are you, you jackass in glasses, trying to give me a bribe?"

The one in glasses, of course, immediately realizes the full extent of his shameful position.

"No," he says, "I took out the money for no reason. I wanted you to hold it while I removed the crates from the scale."

He becomes completely confused, babbles pure nonsense, begins to apologize, and even seems agreeable to having his nose punched.

The weighmaster says:

"For shame. No bribes are taken here. Get your six crates off the scale, they send chills into my heart. But, since they are government crates, why don't you approach that worker over there, he'll reinforce your deficient packaging. As for the money, thank your lucky stars that I am too busy to mess around with you."

Nevertheless he calls over another employee and tells him in a recently insulted voice:

"You know, I have just been offered a bribe. Can you imagine such an absurdity? Now I am sorry I acted hastily and didn't fake taking the money, since now it would be hard to prove."

The other employee answered:

"Yeah, that's too bad. We should have made a big fuss. No way should they be able to think that we still have itchy palms."

The guy with glasses, completely discombobulated, fusses around his crates. He gets them reinforced, and brought into orthodox shape, and again drags them onto the scale.

By then my packaging, too, began to look weak.

And, before it is my turn, I walk over to the worker and ask him to reinforce my questionable packaging, just in case. He wants to charge me eight rubles.

I say to him: "Are you nuts or something, asking eight rubles for three nails?"

He tells me in an intimate voice:

"That's true, I'd do it for three, but you must put yourself in my predicament—see, I've got to share with that crocodile over there."

That's when I figured out the whole set-up.

"You mean to tell me," I say to him, "you split with the weighmaster?"

He now becomes somewhat embarrassed at having spilled the beans, babbles all kinds of nonsense and baloney, mumbles something about miserable pay and high prices, gives me a considerable discount and busies himself with my stuff.

And now my turn comes.

I set my crate onto the scale and admire the sturdy packaging.

The weighmaster says:

"Weak packaging. It won't do."

I say: "Really? I had it reinforced just now. That guy over there, with the pliers, did it."

"Oh, pardon me, pardon me. I apologize. Now your packaging is strong, but it was weak. That always catches my eye. When I am wrong, I am wrong."

So he takes my crate and writes the shipping order.

I read the order and it says: "deficient packaging."

"What are you doing to me," I say to him, "you crooks? With a label like this they'll pilfer everything out of my crate along the way. And the label will not allow me to recover the loss. Now," I tell him, "I see your crooked schemes."

The weighmaster says:

"When I am wrong, I am wrong. I apologize."

He crosses out the label and I go home reflecting along the way about the complex spiritual make-up of my co-citizens, about character rehabilitation, about shrewdness and the unwillingness with which my esteemed co-citizens give up their cushy spots.

When I'm wrong, I'm wrong.

Firewood

Often I brood, in nostalgic mood,
on that hallowed word—firewood.

A. *Blok*

This authentic event took place on Christmas. The newspapers noted in small print in the "Events of the Day" section that it happened at such and such a place and on such and such a date.

But I happen to be an impatient and curious man. The cut and dried lines in a newspaper did not satisfy me.

I hustled over to the address given, found the culprit of this whole incident, wormed my way into his confidence, and asked him to shed a more detailed light on this occurrence.

Over a bottle of beer the entire chain of events was illuminated.

The reader is by nature distrustful. He'll think: "look how smoothly this man lies."

I am not lying, reader. At this very instant, reader, I could look straight into your limpid eyes and say: "I am not lying." And in general, I never lie and always try to write without inventing things. Imagination is not my strong point. And for this reason I don't like to waste my vital juices on some non-existent invention. I know, my dear reader, that life is much more important than literature.

And so, I want you to listen now to this almost Yuletide story.

"Firewood," said my conversation mate, "is a precious item. Particularly when snow is in evidence and the temperature hits lower depths, you can find nothing better in the world than firewood.

"You can even give firewood for birthdays.

"I gave Lisaveta Ivanovna, a cousin of mine, a bundle of firewood for her birthday. And at the end of the party Peter Semenych, that spouse of hers, a hotheaded and irritable son of a bitch, hit me on the head with a log.

" 'This,' he said, 'ain't your 1919 to give people firewood.'

"But, in spite of this, I have not changed my opinion about firewood. Firewood is a precious and sacred item.

"Even in the street, as you walk past, say, a fence, and the cold nips at you, you can't help but stroke the wooden fence.

"And there is a special breed of thief who goes after firewood. A pickpocket, compared to him, is nothing but a small social minnow.

"The firewood thief is a desperado. And you'll never get him on the first try.

"It was by accident that we caught the thief.

"Our firewood was stacked up in the yard. And that communal firewood began to disappear. Every day there would be a shortage of three or four logs. Seryoga Pestikov was the one who fussed about it the most.

" 'We gotta,' he said, 'keep watch, my good folks. Otherwise,' he said, 'there ain't no way we gonna catch the thief.'

"The people agreed. We started keeping watch. We took turns keeping watch, but the logs continued to disappear.

"And so a month went by. Then my nephew, Mishka Vlasov, showed up at my place.

" 'As you know, Uncle,' he said, 'I belong to the Chemist's Union. Seeing that we are related, I can, for a negligible sum, provide you with a dynamite cartridge. And you,' he said, 'stick that dynamite into a log and wait. We, from Petrozavodsk,' he said, 'always do that at home. This throws a scare into the thieves and they lay off stealing from us. It's,' he said, 'a rich idea.'

" 'Go fetch it,' I said, 'you son of a birdbrain. We'll plant it today.'

"He fetched it.

"I carved a slot in a log, put in the cartridge. Covered it up. And nonchalantly tossed the log onto the firewood pile. Then I waited to see what would happen.

"That evening an explosion occurred in the building.

"The folks got frightened to death, 'what the hell is going on,' they wondered, but I knew, and the nephew Mishka knew what the deal was. And the deal was that the dynamite exploded in apartment number four, in the stove of Seryoga Pestikov.

"I said nothing to Seryoga Pestikov about this, I only looked with sadness at his low-life face, his disordered apartment, the piles of bricks instead of the stove, at the broken door, and silently walked out.

"There was one victim. Seryoga's tenant, the invalid Goosev, died from fear. A brick conked him on the noggin.

"As for Seryoga Pestikov and his saintly mother, they are still living among the ruins. And the whole family will, after the New Year's, appear in court for theft and firewood disappearance.

"And only one thing is unfair and annoying: the son of a bitch

Mishka Vlasov claims all the laurels.

"But I will say before the court, 'what do you mean, laurels, if it was I who carved the log and it was I who stuck in the dynamite?'

"Let the court distribute the laurels."

Quality Goods

My friends, the Goosevs, had a German from Berlin living with them. He rented a room. Stayed almost two months.

And he wasn't some kind of Volga German or some other ethnic minority. He was a real, honest to goodness German Berliner. Knew no Russian—zilch. He communicated with his landlords by using his hands and head.

This German dressed dazzlingly, of course. His shirts were clean. His pants smooth. Everything was just so. I tell you, he was a picture.

And when this German was packing to leave, he left his landlords a whole bunch of stuff. An entire heap of overseas wares. All kinds of vials, collars, and little boxes. Nearly two pairs of underpants as well. Also a sweater with hardly any holes. As for small items—both for men's and women's use, there was no end to them.

All this he left piled up in the corner by the wash bowl.

The landlady, Madame Goosev, an honest woman—don't let anyone tell you otherwise, dropped a hint to the Kraut as he was about to leave, like, bitte—schmitte, your herrship, but in your haste you seem to have forgotten to pack these overseas goods.

The Kraut jerked his head. This meant: "Bitte—schmitte, be my guest, take it, what's to talk about, I'm not stingy."

Now the landlords lost no time swooping down on the abandonned merchandise. Goosev even made an itemized list of all the things. And, it goes without saying, he promptly put on the sweater and took possession of the underpants.

Afterwards, he walked around holding the shorts in his hands for two weeks. Proud beyond words, he showed them to everybody and praised the quality of German products.

And the things were, even though well-worn and, in fact, barely holding together, true overseas goods—a pleasure to behold.

There was, by the way, among all those things left behind, something like a flask, or, perhaps, you might call it a canister, with powder in it. The powder was sort of pink and fine. And it had a rather pleasant smell—not unlike lorigan or rose.

After the first few days of joy and jubilation, the Goosevs began to wonder what kind of powder that was. They smelled it, gnashed it between their teeth, tossed a pinch of it into the fire, but learned nothing.

They took it to all their neighbors, showed it to college students and to intelligentsia types, all to no avail.

Many said it was face powder, but some said it was a fine German talcum powder for sprinkling on recently born German kids.

Goosev said:

"I have no use for fine German talc. I don't have any recently born kids. Let it be facial powder. Let me dust my beezer with it every time I shave. For once there'll be a little culture in my life."

So he started shaving and powdering his face. After every shave he walked around pink, resplendent, and nothing short of fragrant.

This, of course, caused much envy and lots of questions.

In response, Goosev strongly endorsed the German manufacturing industry. Warmly, and at length, he praised German goods.

"For how many years," he would say, "did I pollute my face with all kinds of Russian junk, but my day has finally come! And," he would say, "I sumply don't know what I'm going to do when this powder runs out. I guess I'll have to send for another jar. It's such a fine product."

A month later, when the powder was almost all gone, an intellectual friend of Goosev's came to visit. During the evening tea he read the canister. It turned out that it contained a German preparation for discouraging fleas.

Another, less optimistic person would, of course, have been greatly depressed in this situation. And, perhaps, a less optimistic person's kisser would have sprung a lot of psychosomatic pimples and blackheads. But not Goosev.

"That's something," he said. "That's what I call quality goods! What an achievement! Absolutely A-number-one stuff. You can powder your face with it or you can dust fleas with it. It's good for everything. And our domestic products..."

And, after praising the German manufacturing industry some more, he said:

"I'd been wondering all along, you know. The whole time I've been using this powder, not one flea has bitten me. They do bite my wife, Mrs. Goosev. My sons too scratch all the time. Our dog Nina likewise. I, on the other hand—nothing. Those rascally fleas may only be insects, but even they know real quality when they see it. That's really something..."

Goosev's powder has now run out. The fleas, I guess, are biting him again.

Penal Servitude

I tell you, owning a bicycle these days is like doing time on the rock pile.

Yes, it is true, you can get a vast amount of pleasure out of it, physical entertainment, and everything. You can run over a dog, say. Or scare a chicken silly.

Still, despite all this, I've had it with the bicycle. I have become seriously ill on account of that machine, on account of that contraption of mine.

I busted my gut. And now I am receiving outpatient treatment. They've found a hernia on me. I am now, possibly, an invalid. My own contraption did me in.

The truth of the situation is, it is impossible to leave the thing unattended for two minutes without its being swiped. Well, by virtue of that, I was forced to carry the machine on my person during the time not occupied with riding it. On my shoulders.

Sometimes I'd walk into a store with the bike, and I'd force all the customers behind the counter with the wheels. Or else I'd go up on one floor or another to visit friends. Or on business. Or to visit relatives.

Even at the relatives' you sit clutching the handlebars. You never know what kind of mood the relatives are in. I have no way of knowing. One can't crawl inside other people's personalities. They may unscrew the back wheel off or pull the inner tube out. Afterwards they'd say: it was that way.

So, all things considered, it was tough.

It is not altogether clear which of us spent more time riding the other. Me riding the bike, or the bike riding me.

Of course, some pre-war cyclists tried to leave their bicycles in the street. They secured them with every kind of lock. That didn't do any good at all as the bikes would still get taken.

So I had to make allowances for the life-style of the rest of the citizens. Had to carry the machine on my shoulders.

Ordinarily, of course, for a person with a sound psyche, carrying the bike presents no difficulty. Only this time the circumstances messed me up, but good.

I urgently needed collateral for a drink. The inner man was thirsty.

"I've got to put," I thought to myself, "the bite on someone."

It was a good thing I had the bike. I hopped on it and was on my way. Went to a friend's place—found him at home all right, but no money.

And while this friend lived on the third floor, the next one, by contrast, lived on the seventh. I had to run up and then down again with the machine on my back, and by then my tongue hung out.

Next I went to see a relative. On Simbirsk street. My ever-loving aunt.

And she, the nuisance, lived on the sixth floor.

Lugging my contraption, I ascended to the sixth floor. On her door I discovered a note. Said she'd be back in half an hour.

"The old bat," I thought, "sure gets around."

I was greatly upset and, impulsively, walked down again. Sure, I should have waited with the bike upstairs, but I was upset, so I went down. And there I waited for my aunt.

Soon she arrived and took offense because I didn't want to go upstairs with her.

"All I have on me," she said, "is small change. The rest of my money is in the apartment."

I heaved the bicycle on my shoulder, and followed my aunt up. And I could feel hiccups starting up and my tongue wanting to stick out. Nevertheless I made it. Received money in full. Had a bite to fortify my organism. Pumped up a tire and went down.

No sooner did I get down that I discovered that the front door was locked. In her apartment building they lock up at seven.

I didn't say anything at the time, only gnashed my teeth something awful, hefted the bike on my back, and started walking up once more.

I don't know how long it took me to get up. I was practically sleep-walking.

My aunt, the nuisance, laughed as she let me out the back door.

"You ought to keep," she said, "your apparatus upstairs if you are afraid to leave it downstairs."

But then she stopped laughing as she saw a terrible palor spread over my face. And indeed, I stood there swaying, hanging on to the handlebars.

I did get out into the street, though. But I couldn't ride the bike, I was too weak.

And now I suffer the consequences: I am sick because of this penal servitude.

The only comfort I get is thinking that the motorcyclists have it even tougher. They must get mighty emotional about this, I bet!

Another good thing is that they haven't gotten around to building skyscrapers around here yet. Just imagine how many people would be laid low if they had!

"No Waste" Campaign

I don't know, comrades, how this "no waste" campaign works in other cities.

But in the town of Borisov this campaign proved very profitable.

During one short winter, in our enterprise alone, three cords of fir firewood were saved. Not bad, huh?

After all, ten years of such economizing would mean ten cubic meters saved. Over a hundred years we could easily save three bargeloads. In a thousand years, we could readily start our own firewood business.

And what took people so long? How come such a profitable policy wasn't put in circulation earlier? Nobody thought of it, I guess. That's too bad. It was last fall that this "no waste" campaign started.

Our manager's one of the guys. He discusses everything with us and talks to us like we are part of the family. The son of a bitch even bums cigarettes off us.

So this manager came one day and announced:

"Well, boys, here we are, it's begun... Tighten up! See if there's anything we can stop wasting..."

But how and what not to waste, no one knew. So we had a little chat among ourselves as to what to save. Not pay the bookkeeper, that baldheaded old buzzard, perhaps, or something?

The manager said:

"If we don't pay the bookkeeper, boys, the baldheaded old buzzard will run lickety-split to the Labor Protection Bureau. That's no good. Got to come up with something else."

At this time, the cleaning woman Nyusha, bless her heart, brought her coequal feminine point of view up for discussion:

"Considering the current international situation," she said, "and since things in general stink, we could quit," she said, "heating the bathroom. Why consume logs there for nothing? A salon it ain't."

"True enough," we said. "Let the bathroom sit cold. We'll save three cords, maybe. As for its being cold, that's not going to hurt anything. Folks won't linger about when it's nippy in there. This may bring about an actual increase in productivity."

That's what we did. We stopped heating the john and began counting our savings.

We did, in fact, save three cords. We started saving a fourth, but then spring struck.

That was too bad.

We figured that if the damn spring hadn't come, we'd have saved yet another cord.

So spring screwed us up, no question about it. Still, three cords don't grow on trees, either.

As to some dumb pipe or other bursting from freezing, well, it turned out that this pipe had been installed in the dark ages of the tsarist regime. Such pipes should be mercilessly rooted out.

Anyway, till the fall we can easily manage without the pipe. And in the fall, we'll put in a cheap one. A salon it ain't.

The Cup

Ivan Antonovich Fleasky, the house painter, died recently for reasons of health. And his widow, Maria Vassilevna Fleasky, a comely little lady pushing thirty-nine, threw a modest picnic on the fortieth day.

And she invited me too.

"Come," she said, "we'll have a little memorial potluck for the dearly deceased. There'll be," she said, "no chickens or fried gooses, nor should you expect any pâté de liverwurst. But you can swill tea to your heart's content—as much as you want—and you can even take some home with you."

I said:

"Although tea is not what you might call a big attraction, I guess I'll come. Ivan Antonovich Fleasky treated me friendly-like and even whitewashed my ceiling once free of charge."

"Well," she said, "all the more reason for you to come."

And so on Thursday I went.

There was a mob of people there. Relatives of every kind. Including the brother-in-law, Peter Antonovich Fleasky. An obnoxious gent with a little black moustache sticking up. Sat right in front of the the watermelon. And had nothing better to do, see, but slice pieces of the watermelon off with a penknife and eat them.

As for me, I consumed one cup of tea, and didn't feel like having more. My heart, you know, wasn't in it. And anyway, their tea wasn't all that great, I must say—there was a hint of dishrag in it. So I took the teacup and set it aside.

Only I set it aside just a trifle carelessly. There was a sugar bowl standing there. And it was against that sugar bowl that I struck the piece of crockery, against the handle. And the dumb cup, damn it to hell, up and cracked.

I thought they wouldn't notice. They did, the scoundrels.

The widow replied:

"Looks like you clinked that cup, my good man, didn't you?"

I said:

"It's nothing, Maria Vassilevna Fleasky. It'll hold together for some time yet."

But the brother-in-law, stuffed with watermelon to the gills, answered:

"What do you mean 'nothing?' How do you like that? He calls it nothing. A widow invites them to the party, and they smash the widow's objects."

Meanwhile Maria Vassilevna kept examining the cup and getting more and more upset.

"In a household," she said, "cup-breaking is ruin pure and simple. One guest," she said, "will bust a cup, another one will break the spout clean off the teapot, the third one 'll stick a napkin in his pocket. Where will that leave me?"

The brother-in-law, the parasite, answered:

"What's there," he said, "to talk about? The only thing to do with guests like that," he said, "is to bust them in the kisser with a watermelon."

I made no reply to this. I only turned awfully pale and said:

"I, comrade brother-in-law," I said, "find it rather offensive to hear about the kisser. I, comrade brother-in-law," I said, "wouldn't allow my own mother to bust my kisser with a watermelon. And anyway," I said, "your tea smells of dishrag. Some fancy invitation," I said. "If I broke three teacups," I said, "and one coffee mug it wouldn't be enough for bums like you."

That, of course, caused a lot of noise and commotion.

It was the brother-in-law who made the biggest uproar. All that watermelon he had eaten must have gone to his head.

And the widow too was palpitating with rage.

"It ain't a habit of mine," she said, "to steep dishrags in the tea. Maybe you make tea that way at home, and then pretend that others do it too. The house painter Ivan Antonovich," she said, "must be tossing in his grave from such aggravating words... There's no way now," she said, "I'll let you get away with it, you son of a sea cook."

I made no reply to this, I only said:

"Phooey to you all," I said, "and phooey to the brother-in-law."

And then I got out of there as fast as I could.

Two weeks after these facts I received a court summons in the Fleasky case.

I appeared before the court more than a little surprised.

The people's judge heard the case and said:

"All the courts these days," she said, "are overflooded with every imaginable kind of case, and now this, to top it all. Pay," she said, "this citizen two bits and clear the air in the courtroom."

I said:

"I have no objections to paying, but, as a matter of principle, let them give me the cracked cup."

The widow said:

"Take the cup. I hope you choke on it."

And the next day, see, their janitor Simon brought the cup over. What's more, it was cracked three other places on purpose.

I didn't say anything to this, I only commented:

"Tell your scum," I said, "that now I'll drag them through the courts."

Because indeed, when my dander is up, I am capable of going as far as the tribunal.

The Passenger

Why the heck do they let the passengers ride to Moscow on the third shelf? After all, it is a baggage rack, isn't it? Let the baggage ride on the baggage shelf, not travelers.

Culture and enlightenment, they say! So, for instance, they fasten diesel engines to the trains better to travel in them. Yet all the while they allow such dense hickdom in the railroad cars.

You can get your coconut cracked, for Pete's sake! If you fall down, that is. You do fall down, you know, not up.

And it so happens that I had no need at all to go to Moscow. It so happens that that son of a bitch Vaska Bochkov suckered me into this lovely trip.

"Here," he said, "take this free pass. Go to Moscow if you feel like it."

"My bosom buddy," I said, "what in Sam Hill would I want to go to Moscow for? I simply don't feel like going to Moscow," I said. "I have no kith and even less kin in Moscow. I don't have, my good buddy," I said, "even a place to stay in that there Moscow."

But he said:

"Go just for the fun of it. It's free, after all. One time in your life," he said, "a bit of luck comes knocking at your door, and you, blockhead, want to give it the bum's rush."

So Saturday going on Sunday I left.

I entered the car. Sat down on the edge of the bench. And rode along. I rode three miles and my stomach began growling something fierce, yet there was nothing to eat.

"Boy," I thought, "Vaska Bochkov, you son of a bitch, what a long trip you suckered me into. I'd just as soon be sitting somewhere on dry land in a beerhall than be traveling back and forth."

Meanwhile, quite a few people had collected in the car.

There, by the window, for instance, was a gent with a beard.

Here, right next to me, as luck would have it, was a little old lady. And what an ornery, poisonous little old lady she turned out to be—she kept shoving me with her elbow.

"Look at him sprawling," she said, "damn him. I don't have room to breathe or sigh."

I said:

"Little old lady," I said, "you God's own little puffball, quit shoving. I am not," I said, "riding here because I feel like it. Vaska Bochkov," I said, "suckered me into it."

She didn't show any compassion.

Meanwhile, night set in. The sparks from the diesel fell like rain. There was beauty and nature all around. Only I didn't feel like gazing at nature. "The nice thing to do," I thought, "would be to lie down and pull up the covers."

But, as far as I could see, there was no place to lie down. All the seats were taken solid.

I spoke to the passengers:

"Citizens," I said, "let me at least sit in the middle. I might fall sitting here, on the edge. I'm going clear to Moscow."

"Everyone around here," they answered, "is going to Moscow. Nor does this train have reserved seats. Sit where you sat."

I sat. And rode. I rode another three miles—my leg went numb. I stood up. And that's when I caught sight of the third shelf. A basket was riding on it.

"Citizens," I said, "what's this, for Pete's sake? A man has to sit all twisted, and his legs get numb, while here we have things... A man," I said, "is, after all, more important than things... Whose basket," I said, "is this? Take it away."

The little old lady got up groaning. Started reaching up to get the basket.

"Neither day or night," she said, "will you leave me in peace, damn you. Here," she said, "you graven image, clamber up there into the stratosphere. God willing," she said, "you'll get your coconut cracked as night descends upon us."

Up I went.

So I climbed up there, rode three miles, and dozed off soundly.

Suddenly wham!—there was a nasty jerk sideways and I went tumbling down. I realized that I was falling.

"What a way to wake up," I thought, "falling down."

Then crash—I got clobbered in the side, on the head, in the gut, on the arm... I had landed.

It is a good thing my leg caught on the second shelf—that softened the blow somewhat.

So there I was, sitting on the floor feeling my noggin to see if it was still there. It was.

And there was a lot of noise in the car all around me. That noise was caused by the passengers shouting as they were afraid their things might get stolen in the confusion.

The noise brought along a brigade of train personnel with a lantern.

The chief conductor asked:

"Who fell?"

I said:

"I fell. From the baggage shelf. I am going," I said, "to Moscow. Vaska Bochkov," I said, "suckered me into this lovely trip."

The chief conductor said:

"At Bologoe the passangers regularly tumble down. It's a mighty abrupt stop."

I said: "It is rather offensive to a man who has just fallen down to hear about this. It would be better," I said, "if the railroad personnel kept people from riding on the top shelf. And if a passenger starts climbing up there, they should push him off or reason with him—like, don't go up there, citizen, as you might possibly tumble down."

And now the little old lady set up a howl:

"He scrunched my basket with his noggin."

I said:

"Man is more important than a basket. You can," I said," buy a basket. The noggin," I said, "is, after all, for free."

So everyone yelled for a while, moaned for a while, they bandaged my head with a rag, and, without stopping the train, we rode on.

I reached Moscow. Got off the train. Sat around the station for a spell.

Drank four glasses of water at the fountain. And headed back.

Did my head ever throb and buzz! And it was filled with all kinds of obscene thoughts.

"O-oh boy," I thought, "if I could only lay my hands on Vaska Bochkov right now, I'd sure knock the stuffing out of him. What a trip," I thought, "he suckered me into."

I reached Leningrad. Got out of the train. Drank a glass of water at the fountain and went on my way swaying a little.

Four Days

The German war and all those trenches and stuff—we are now, citizens, paying the price for these things. Because of them we are all now sick and unhealthy.

Some people's nerves are shot, others have cramps or something in their bellies, some people's hearts are not as arhythmical as would be desirable. These are the consequences.

As to my health, of course, I can't complain. I'm healthy. I eat pretty good. And my sleep is beneficial. Yet, every minute I anticipate that them there trenches'n stuff will take their toll.

So, for instance, not too long ago I got up from my bed. And I was putting on, I can remember this as if it were yesterday, my boot. And the spouse, she said to me:

"Your face, Vanya," she said, "looks kind of gray, or something, today. You seem to have," she said, "an unhealthy rufous color."

I looked in the mirror. True enough, the color was desperately rufous, and the face begged to be hit with a brickbat.

"Son of a gun!" I thought, "the trenches'n stuff are doing their thing. Perhaps my heart or some other organ isn't beating as it should. That's the reason, maybe, I am turning gray."

I felt my pulse. Though slowly, it was functioning. Some pain, however, started up inside. And something began to throb.

Sadly I dressed and, without having tea, went to work.

So I came to work. "If some bastard," I thought, "says anything about the way I look or the color of my face, I'll go see a doctor—no two ways about it. You see it all the time: a man lives and lives and suddenly poof!—he's dead.Happens every day."

At five to eleven—I remember it as if it were yesterday—the senior machine tool operator Zhitkov walked up to me and said:

"Ivan Fyodorovich, my good fellow, what is the matter with you? Your appearance is altogether desperate. You have an unhealthy muddy appearance."

These words cut me to the quick.

"There goes my health acrumbling, by gosh," I thought. "It has caught up with me."

And again it started throbbing inside me, making me woozy. I tell you, I barely made it home. I just about called an ambulance.

So I made it home. Collapsed on the bed. And lay there. The wife started bawling from grief. The neighbors came, tsk-tsked.

"My," they said, "some appearance you have, Ivan Fyodorovich. Yes, indeed. What you have is not a face, but rufous pure and simple."

These words upset me even worse. I lay on my back and couldn't sleep.

In the morning I got up as out of sorts as a son of a bitch. And had the communal physician called over.

The communal physician came and said: "Malingering."

I almost beat the physician up for these words.

"I'll show you malingering," I said. "I may splurge to the tune of three rubles and go visit the professor himself."

So I started getting ready to go to the professor. I put on clean underwear. Started to shave. I ran the razor down the cheek, got the soap off, lo and behold, the cheek was white, healthy, with a lively pink flush on it.

I quickly started rubbing my face with a washcloth—the gray rufous color came clean off.

The wife came in and said:

"I guess, Vanya, it's been a week since you took water to your face, eh?"

I said:

"A week? That can't be. What a dumb thing to say, you silly goose. But," I said, "four days or so, that, I guess is about right."

The thing is, our kitchen is so cold and uncomfortable. One just doesn't feel like washing there. And when all the moaning and groaning started, well, you understand, washing was the furthest thing from my mind. All I worried about was making it to the bed.

So I immediately washed up, shaved, hung a necktie on and, fresh as a daisy, went to see a friend.

Right away the pains, too, seemed to diminish. And the heart beat fairly well.

The Bathhouse vs. the People

At one time we wrote something about bathhouses. We signalled the danger. A naked man, we said, has no place to put his claim checks, and so on.

Several years have passed since then.

The problem we brought up caused lively discussion in the bath and laundry industry. As a result, in some bathhouses they have installed special boxes where the client can put his clothing, such as it is. Then the box is locked with a key. And the client, joy in his heart, hurries off to wash. There he ties the key to the basin. Or, if worst comes to worst, doesn't let it out of his hand. And washes as best as he can.

Briefly, in spite of all this, the following events unfolded in a Leningrad bathhouse.

A technician, having washed, decided, of course, to get dressed. And suddenly he discovered, to his horror, that his whole wardrobe had been stolen. Except that the thief, bless his kind heart, left him the vest, cap, and belt.

The poor technician was flabbergasted. There he was, standing by his box with nothing on, contemplating his dim prospects. That's all he could do, stand by his box and gesture with his hands. The man was in shock.

Yet—he was a technician. Not without education. And he simply couldn't imagine how he would get home. He could just barely keep on his feet.

Eventually, however, he unthinkingly put on his vest and cap, took the belt in his hand, and in this, one might say, absolutely surrealistic attire, began walking around the locker room completely discombobulated.

Some of the customers said:

"Nary a day goes by in this bathhouse without somebody getting robbed."

The technician, his head spinning, began to speak in some pre-revolutionary dialect featuring the word "gentlemen." It must be that all the excitement caused him to lose certain traits of his newly acquired personality.

He said:

"I am mostly interested to know, gentlemen, how I am going to get home."

Some of the yet-unwashed said:

"Call the manager. He'll have to figure something out."

The technician said in a weak voice:

"Gentlemen, please summon the manager for me."

Thereupon the attendant, wearing nothing but rolled-up pants, rushed to the door and soon reappeared with the manager in tow. At this point everyone present suddenly noticed that the manager was a woman. The technician took the cap off his head and said musingly:

"Gentlemen, what's happening here, for goodness' sake? Things are going from bad to worse. We were all fervently hoping to see a man in this situation, but instead a woman arrives. Can you believe it? To have managers of this kind in a men's bathhouse," he said, "is nothing less than... than a magnetic anomaly."

And, covering himself with the cap, he sat down on a bench exhausted.

Other men said:

"To have a manager who's a woman, that's indeed a magnetic anomaly."

The manager said:

"To you, I may be a magnetic anomaly. But over there, across the hall, is a ladies' section. And over there," she said, "I'm far from being anything like a magnetic anomaly."

The technician tugged at his vest and said:

"Madam, it was not our intention to insult you. So there's no reason for you to be in a snit. You'd better figure out what I'm going to wear home."

The manager said:

"Before me, of course, there were male managers here. And they were very good in the performance of their duties here, in this section, but over there, in the ladies' section, they would all go bananas. They'd pop in there much too often. So now men are seldom appointed to this post. They appoint mostly women. And, as far as I'm concerned, I come here only when required, or when something's been filched, and I don't lose my head over it. As for me constantly running into insults here, and every bather calling me without fail a magnetic anomaly, I'm warning you all that the next guy to insult me during the performance of my duties will be taken to the police station. Now. What's happened here?"

The technician said:

"Gentlemen, why is she in such a snit? I wish she'd go to hell. Here I am, unable to foresee how I am going to get home without pants, and she won't allow me to call her a magnetic anomaly. What's more, she's threatening me with the police. No, it would be so much nicer if the manager were a man. He at least could lend me some spare pants. This business of a woman manager—it's the last straw. And I am now convinced, gentlemen, that I'm not going to leave this bathhouse for several days, you just wait and see."

The onlookers said to the manager:

"Listen, madam. Maybe you have a husband here at the bathhouse. And maybe he has a pair of spare trousers. Then why don't you let this gentleman wear them for a time. He's terribly upset, you know. And he can't seem to figure out a way to get home."

The manager said:

"In the ladies' section there's peace and quiet, while in this half every day something like a volcanic eruption takes place. No, gentlemen, I refuse to be a manager here. My husband works in Kursk. So, of course, there's no question about any pants of his. Particularly in view of the fact that this is the second complaint of theft today. It's a good thing they stole small stuff the first time. Otherwise, I'd be pestered about trousers twice in a row. Anyway, gentlemen, I'll tell you what: if one of you has spare pants of any kind, give them to the gentleman. I can't bear to look at the poor fellow. I'm getting a migraine from all these upheavals."

The attendant said:

"All right, once again I'll lend out my spare pants. But it's time we got an official pair. We often have thefts, and over this last month alone they've just about worn my pants out. One guy borrows them, then another. And they are my own."

Thereupon the attendant gave the technician a pair of calico pants and one of the bathers gave him a windbreaker and a pair of slippers to wear. And soon our friend, suppressing sobs with difficulty, arrayed himself in this outlandish get-up. And he left the bathhouse completely dazed.

After he had left, someone suddenly shouted:

"Look, here's someone else's spare vest, and one sock."

Then everyone gathered around the newly-found articles.

One man said:

"The thief, probably, dropped them. Take a good look at the vest. Maybe there's something in the pockets. People often carry papers in vest pockets."

They turned the pockets inside out and suddenly discovered a certificate. It was a pass issued to one Selifanov, who worked at the Central Garment Shop.

Everyone realized that the thief's tracks had now been uncovered.

Thereupon the manager briskly called the police and two hours later a search was carried out at this Selifanov's place.

Selifanov was greatly surprised and said:

"You, gentlemen, have gone off your rocker. I myself had things stolen at this bathhouse today. I even made out a complaint. As for this vest of mine, the thief must have dropped it."

Everyone apologized to Selifanov and said to him:

"It was just a misunderstanding."

But suddenly the manager of the garment shop where Selifanov worked said:

"Yes, I am sure you were victimized at the bathhouse. But tell me, where'd you get this piece of tweed I see in your trunk? That tweed is from our shop. It was missing. And you probably took it. It's a good thing I came along for the search out of curiosity."

Selifanov began babbling at this point and soon confessed to the theft of the piece of tweed.

Thereupon he was instantly arrested. And thus ends our bathhouse story, and other matters begin. But we better not say anything on these so as not to confuse different subjects.

The Adventures of a Monkey

In one of our southern towns there was a zoo. It was a small zoo consisting of one tiger, two crocodiles, three snakes, a zebra, an ostrich, and one simian, or, speaking plainly, a monkey. And, of course, small stuff of various description—birds, little fish, frogs, and other insignificant fry from the animal world.

When the Fascists bombed this town at the beginning of the war, one bomb fell directly into the zoo. And it exploded there with a huge, deafening boom, much to the surprise of all the animals.

As a result, the three snakes were killed—all at once—which, perhaps, was not a particularly depressing fact. And, unfortunately, the ostrich.

The other beasts were not harmed. They, as the saying goes, got off with nothing worse than a scare.

Among the animals it was the simian, the monkey, who was frightened the worst. Its cage was knocked over by the air blast. The cage fell off its stand and the side wall broke. And this monkey fell out of its cage directly onto the path.

It fell onto the path, but did not remain lying there motionless, following the example of humans who are accustomed to military operations. Just the opposite. It immediately climbed a tree. From there it hopped onto a fence. From the fence into the street. And started running like a bat out of hell.

While running, it probably thought: "Gee, if they are going to toss bombs around here, leave me out of it." And so it kept running through the town's streets as hard as it could.

It ran through the whole town. Came to a highway. And continued running along the highway away from the town. Well, what do you expect? It was a monkey, not a human. It didn't know what was what. It could see no sense in staying in the town.

So it ran, and ran, and it got tired. It was utterly exhausted. It climbed into a tree. Ate a fly to restore its strength. Also two grubs. Then it fell asleep right there, on the branch, where it sat.

But at this time a military vehicle came along the road. The driver saw the monkey in the tree. He was surprised. Quietly he stole up on the monkey. And covered it with his overcoat. Then he put it in his car. And he thought:

"I'd better give it to some friends, rather than leave it here to die from hunger, cold, and other deprivations."

And so he drove on with the monkey in his car.

He arrived in the town of Borisov. Went about his business. And he left the monkey in the car. He said to it:

"You wait for me here, sweetheart. I'll be right back."

But the monkey didn't wait. It crawled out of the car through a broken window and went for a stroll in the streets.

And so, there it was, minding its own business while having a stroll, a promenade, its tail to the wind. The folks, of course, were amazed to see it and wanted to catch it. But catching it was no easy matter. The monkey was quick, nimble, and could run fast on its four hands. So they never caught it, only needlessly ran it ragged.

It got tired from all that useless running around and, of course, felt a desire to eat.

But where in this town could it find anything to eat? In the streets there was nothing particularly edible. It couldn't very well visit a cafeteria, tail and all, could it? Or a cooperative store. Particularly since it didn't have any money. No discount. It had no food coupons. It was a nightmare.

Nevertheless it did stop at a cooperative store. It sensed that there were goodies to be had there. And just then, in that store, they were distributing vegetables to the population—carrots, rutabaga, and cucumbers.

So it visited the store. It observed a long line standing there. No, it didn't stand in line. Nor did it begin elbowing its way to the counter. It ran up to the saleslady right over the heads of the customers. It hopped onto the counter. It didn't even ask how much a bunch of carrots was. And then, as they say, it took it on the lam. It ran out of the store quite satisfied with its purchase. Well, what do you expect from a monkey, it didn't know what was what. It could see no sense in going on without provisions.

This visit, of course, caused much noise, shouting, and commotion in the store. The customers screamed. The saleslady, who was weighing out rutabaga, was so startled, she nearly fainted. Well, wouldn't you be frightened if, instead of the usual, normal customer, you found yourself next to something hairy, with a tail? Something that doesn't pay money to boot?

The folks rushed out into the street after the monkey. But the monkey ran merrily along nibbling at a carrot—having a snack. It didn't know what was what.

And so at the head of the crowd ran the boys. Behind them the grown-ups. And, bringing up the rear, ran a policeman blowing his whistle.

Suddenly, out of nowhere, a dog jumped out. And it too took after the monkey. And, while doing so, it not only yelped and barked, but it kept trying in earnest to grab the monkey with its teeth.

Our monkey ran faster. As it ran, it no doubt thought:

"Goodness me, leaving the zoo was not such a good idea. I could breathe a lot easier in my cage. I'll most certainly return to the zoo the first chance I get."

And so the monkey ran as fast as it could, but the dog kept up with it and was on the point of catching it.

The monkey then hopped onto a fence that happened to be there. And when the dog jumped up trying at least to grab the monkey by the foot, the monkey hit the dog with the carrots in the nose with all its might. And the blow was so painful that the dog yowled and ran home with its busted nose. It was, probably, thinking:

"No sir, citizens, I'd rather be lying home in peace than be catching a monkey for you and experiencing such utter unpleasantness."

In brief, the dog ran off, and the monkey jumped into the courtyard.

And at that time, a teenage boy, Alyosha Popov by name, was chopping wood there, in the yard.

So there he was, chopping wood, when suddenly he saw the monkey. And he loved monkeys. All his life he had been dreaming of having a monkey of one kind of another as a pet. And suddenly his fondest wish was answered!

Alyosha took off his jacket and with this jacket he covered the monkey which had sought refuge in a corner in the stairway.

The boy brought it home. Fed it. Gave it some tea. And the monkey was very happy. But not perfectly happy. That was because Alyosha's grandmother had taken an immediate dislike to the monkey. She yelled at it and even wanted to hit it on the paw. All this because while they were drinking tea, Granny had put her much bitten candy down on the saucer, and the monkey had grabbed Granny's piece of candy and stuffed it into its mouth. Well, what do you expect, it was a monkey, not a human. If a human took anything, he'd at least make sure Granny wasn't looking. But the monkey did it right there, before Granny's eyes. And, of course, almost brought Grandma to tears.

Grandma said: "In general it is quite unpleasant to have some kind of a macaque with a tail living around the apartment. It will keep startling me with its inhuman appearance. It will jump on me in the dark. It will gobble my candy. No, I most definitely refuse to live in the same apartment with a monkey. One of us must reside in a zoological garden. Must I really move out to the zoo? No, better let the monkey be there. And I'll go on living in my apartment."

Alyosha said to his grandmother:

"No, Grandma, you don't have to go to the zoo. I guarantee that the monkey won't eat anything else of yours.

"I will bring it up like a human being. I will teach it to eat with a teaspoon. And drink tea from a cup. As to its jumping, I can't very well forbid it to climb up onto the light-fixture hanging from the ceiling. From there, of course, it might jump onto your head. But, the main thing is, you should not get frightened if this happens. Because it is nothing more than a harmless monkey who was accustomed in Africa to hop and jump."

The next day Alyosha went to school. And he asked his grandma to keep an eye on the monkey. But the grandma had no intention of keeping an eye on it. She thought:

"The very idea, me looking after some sort of a monster."

And, with such thoughts, she went and on purpose dozed off in the armchair.

And now our monkey crawled out through the open transom and then ran out into the street. And started walking along the sunny side. Maybe it simply felt like having a stroll, or, who knows, maybe it wanted to drop in at the store once more and there buy something for itself. Not for cash, on the cuff.

Just then an old man happened by. The disabled Gavrilich. He was on his way to the bathhouse. He was carrying in his hand a small basket where he had his soap and a change of clothes.

He saw the monkey and at first couldn't believe his eyes that it was a monkey. He thought he was seeing things as he had just drunk a tankard of beer.

So there he was, looking at the monkey with amazement. And the monkey was looking at him. It was, perhaps, thinking:

"What kind of scarecrow is this, with a basket in hand?"

Eventually Gavrilich realized that it was a real monkey, not an imagined one. And then he thought:

"Why don't I catch it? I'll take it to the flea market tomorrow and sell it for a hundred rubles. And for that money I'll drink ten tankards of beer in a row."

And, with this thought, he began chasing the monkey and saying:

"Here, kitty, kitty, kitty... Come over here."

Yes, he knew it was not a cat, but he couldn't figure out in what language he should talk to it. It took him a little while to realize that it was the highest creature in the animal kingdom. And then he pulled a lump of sugar out of his pocket, showed it to the monkey, bowed, and said:

"Would you, lovely simian, care to partake of a lump of sugar?"

The simian said:

"Don't mind if I do..."

Actually, though, it didn't say anything at all because it didn't know how to speak. It simply walked up, took the lump of sugar and began eating it.

Gavrilich took it in his hands and put it in his basket. And it was warm and cozy in the basket. And the monkey didn't try to jump out of there. Perhaps it thought:

"Let this old chump carry me in his basket. This is rather amusing."

At first Gavrilich intended to take it home. But on second thought he didn't feel like returning home. And so he went to the bathhouse taking the monkey with him. He thought:

"It's even better this way, my taking it to the bathhouse. I'll wash it there. It will be nice and clean and cuddly. I'll tie a ribbon around its neck. And then they'll give me more for it at the flea market."

By and by he arrived at the bathhouse with his monkey. And began washing, both himself and the monkey.

And there, in the bathhouse, it was very warm, exactly like Africa. And our monkey was very pleased with such a warm atmosphere. But not perfectly pleased. Because Gavrilich soaped it up, and soap got into its mouth. Soap, of course, tastes bad, but not so bad as to scream, scratch, and refuse to wash. Anyway, the monkey began to spit, but now soap got into its eye. And that made the simian go completely out of its mind. It bit Gavrilich's finger, tore itself away from his grasp and, like a bat out of hell, ran out of the bathhouse.

It jumped into the room where people undress. And there it

threw a scare into one and all. After all, nobody could know that it was a monkey. All they could see was something round, white, covered with foam. It rushed first onto the couch. Then onto the water heater. From the water heater onto a crate. From the crate onto somebody's head. And once again onto the water heater.

Some nervous customers screamed and began running out of the bathhouse. And the monkey also ran out. And went down the stairs.

At the bottom of the stairs was the cashier's box with a window. The monkey jumped into the window thinking that it would be more peaceful there, and, most important, there would be no crowds, and none of the rushing about. But there was a fat lady cashier sitting in the box and she gasped and started screeching. And she ran out of the cashier's box shouting:

"Help! I think a bomb fell into my cashier's box. Does anyone have a tranquilizer?"

Our monkey was tired of all this yelling. It jumped out of the cashier's box and ran down the street.

And so, there it was, running down the street, all wet, covered with lather, and people were again running after it. Ahead of everybody else ran the boys. Behind them the adults. Behind the adults the policeman. And behind the policeman our senile Gavrilich, barely dressed, his boots in his hand.

At this point, out of nowhere, a dog jumped out, the same one that chased it the previous day.

Seeing it, the monkey thought:

"Well, citizens, now my cause is completely hopeless."

But this time the dog didn't take up the chase. The dog only looked at the running monkey, felt a sharp pain in its nose, and decided against running. It even turned away. It probably reflected:

"No percentage in running after monkeys—this is the only nose I have."

But even though it had turned away, it gave a few angry barks as if to say:

"Run along, but be aware that I'm here."

Meanwhile, the boy Alyosha Popov, on returning from school, didn't find his darling monkey at home. He was very upset. Tears even welled up in his eyes. He thought he'd never see his sweet beloved little monkey again.

And so, out of boredom and despondency, he went out in the street. And started walking down the street full of melancholy.

Suddenly he looked up and saw people running. Now, at first he didn't think that they were running after his monkey. He figured they were running thanks to an air raid alarm. But then he saw his little monkey, all wet, covered with soap. He rushed to it, took it in his arms. And held it tight so as not to let anybody take it.

And then all the people stopped running and surrounded the boy.

But now the senile Gavrilich stepped out of the crowd. And, showing everybody his bitten finger, he said:

"Citizens, don't allow this kid to hold in his arms my little monkey, which I intend to sell tomorrow at the flea market. I tell you, it is my own monkey, the one that bit me on the finger. Take a look at this swollen finger of mine. This is the proof that I am telling the truth."

The boy Alyosha Popov said:

"No, this is not his monkey, it is my monkey. You could see how willingly it came into my arms. And this also is the proof that I am telling the truth."

But now yet another man stepped out of the crowd—the driver who had brought the monkey in his car. He said:

"No, this monkey is not yours, and not yours. It is my monkey because I brought it. But I am going back to my military unit and will, therefore, give the monkey to the person who is holding it lovingly in his arms, and not to the person who callously wishes to sell it at the flea market for the sake of his booze. The monkey belongs to the boy."

All the folks clapped their hands when they heard this. And Alyosha Popov, beaming with happiness, hugged the monkey even tighter. And triumphantly carried it home.

As to Gavrilich with his bitten finger, he went back to the bathhouse to finish his washing.

And ever since the monkey has been living with the boy Alyosha Popov. It still lives with him. Recently I was in the town of Borisov. And I made it a point to visit Alyosha to see what kind of life it had at his place. Oh, it has a fine life! It does not run away from home. It has become very obedient. It wipes its nose with a handkerchief. And it does not take other people's candy. So that even the grandmother is now happy and no longer intends to move to the zoo.

When I entered Alyosha's room, the monkey was sitting at the table. It looked as important as a box-office lady at the movies. And it was eating rice porridge with a teaspoon.

Alyosha said to me:

"I brought it up like a human, and all the children, and to some extent even the adults, can take example from it."

The Terrible Night

You write and write, and no one knows why you write.

The reader, I bet, will smile knowingly at this point. What about the money, he'll say. You do get money, you son of a gun, don't you, he'll say. It's hard to believe how quickly they grow fat and sassy, he'll say.

Ah, my esteemed reader! What's money? So you get money, so you buy some firewood, you buy your wife a pair of overshoes or something, and that's about it. There is no peace of mind to be found in money, nor a cosmic idea.

And yet, if this petty mercenary motive were removed too, this author would send all of literature packing. He'd quit writing. And he'd smash his pen to smithereens.

So help me.

A weird breed of readers we have nowadays. They snatch up French and American novels, but won't touch our home grown Russian literature with a ten-foot pole. They are keen, don't you see, on there being some sort of impetuous flight of fancy in a book, some sort of plot—God only knows what kind of plot.

And where would I get all this?

Where does one get this impetuous flight of fancy if Russian reality isn't like that at all?

And if you have the revolution in mind, well, there is a catch there too. Sure, there's impetuousness there. And there's majestic fancy. But go ahead, try to describe it. Wrong, they'll say. Incorrect. No scientific approach to the problem, they'll say. Your ideology, they'll say, is nothing to write home about.

And where do I get this approach? I ask you, where do I get this scientific approach and ideology if I was born into a middle-class family and to this day I cannot suppress my petty-bourgeois mercenary interests and my adoration of, say, flowers, curtains, and overstuffed chairs?

Ah, my esteemed reader! You'll never know what misery it is to be a Russian writer.

A foreigner can write whatever he pleases, it's like water off a duck's back—runs right off. He'll dish out impetuous fancy for you, and he'll stick something in about wild animals, and he'll send his hero to the moon in a cannonball of some kind...

And it's O.K.

But just try to barge into our literature with something like that. Just try, say, to send our engineer, Klutzkin, Boris Petrovich, to the moon in a cannonball. They'll bury you in ridicule. They'll be offended. "Man, look at the hogwash the bum's peddling," they'll say.

And so you write, fully aware of your hopelessness. And you get no consolation either.

Fame you might say. Well, what about fame? If you think about fame, then what is fame, pray tell? It so happens we don't know what twist the general history of the world may take and how the Earth will turn out from, so to speak, the geological point of view.

The author has recently read in a work by a German philosopher, you see, that our entire life and the flourishing of our culture are, supposedly, nothing more than an interglacial period.

The author confesses: quivers ran down his spine as he read this.

Indeed. Just imagine, reader... Step back for a second from your daily worries and picture this: before us, there existed some kind of life and some kind of advanced culture and then they were wiped out. And now they are flourishing once more and once more absolutely everything will be wiped out. We may not be involved in it, but still the annoying feeling of something transitory, nonever-lasting, accidental, and constantly changing compels us over and over again to rethink our whole life completely anew.

Suppose you wrote a manuscript. The spelling alone almost did you in, not to mention style, and then, say in five hundred years, a mammoth or some other beast steps on your manuscript with its huge foot, pokes it with its tusk, sniffs it and rejects it as inedible junk.

That's why I say that nothing brings you any consolation. Money doesn't, nor fame, nor honors. All that's left is sheer annoyance at your own literature.

But what can you do? Life is funny that way. Existence here on earth can get pretty dreary.

Suppose, for instance, you go out of town, into the fields... Out there in the country you'll see some miserable little house or other. A fence. Quite dreary. A cow might be standing there—so dreary as to drive you to tears... Its side is all covered with dung... It swishes its tail. Chews. A peasant woman wearing the usual gray kerchief sits by the house doing something with her hands. A rooster walks nearby.

My goodness, how dreary!

A towheaded peasant resembling an ambulatory plant might stroll up. He'll walk up to the woman, look with his clear eyes reminiscent of glass beads to see what the woman is doing. He'll hiccup, scratch one leg with the other, yawn. "Might as well hit the sack," he'll say. "Ain't nothin' goin' 'round here..." And he'll go to sleep.

And you keep saying "impetuous fancy, if you please."

Come on, gentlemen, comrade gentlemen! Where am I to get it? How am I going to fit it into this reality? Tell me! Be so kind as to help me out, I beg of you.

And should you go to the city where bright streetlights shine, where citizens fully aware of their human greatness walk every which way, it'll again be dreary. And no impetuous fancy.

So they walk.

All right, reader, take the trouble, try to follow this man: all you'll find is nonsense.

It'll turn out he is on his way to borrow three rubles, or else is going on a date.

He'll arrive, sit down facing his girlfriend, say something about love to her, or, perhaps, he won't say anything at all, he'll simply put his hand on the lady's knee and peer into her eyes.

Or maybe he'll arrive at a friend's home, stay there a while. He'll enjoy a cup of tea; he'll look at his reflection in the samovar and smile to himself—get a load of the funny warped face. He'll drip some jam on the tablecloth and then leave. He'll slap his hat on the side of his head and leave.

And if you ask the son of a bitch what he came for, what is the cosmic idea and what benefit to humanity there is in his coming there, he won't know it himself.

In this particular case, of course, in this dreary picture of city life the author chose little people, insignificant people like himself, and not important public officials or, say, workers in education, who do indeed walk around the city to attend to God knows what important public affairs and circumstances.

The author didn't have such people in mind at all when he spoke about ladies' knees, for instance, or simply about the way they looked at their mugs in the samovar.

The author made the preceding disclaimer because he is looking far ahead and wishes to scold in good time those overzealous critics who will try, out of sheer mischief, to catch the author distorting provincial reality.

No, we are not distorting reality. Nobody pays us money to do that, esteemed comrades.

None of this, though, will change a thing. And the above watercolor of our provincial life will remain unchanged.

It's sad.

You see, the author used to know one such city person. He lived quietly, the way most people live. He ate and drank, and he put his hand on his girlfriend's knee, and he peered into her eyes, and he dripped jam onto the tablecloth, and borrowed three rubles with little intention of ever returning them.

It is about this man that the author will write his very short story. But perhaps the story will not be about this man at all, but rather about the silly and insignificant adventure for which the man suffered compulsory payment of fines in the amount of twenty-five rubles.

Should I dilute this occurrence with fancy? Should I create an entertaining little nuptial intrigue around it? No! Let the French write about that. We will proceed slowly, we will creep forward one step at a time, just like Russian reality.

And the cheerful reader who is looking for a brisk and impetuous flight of fancy and expects spicy details and occurrences is wholeheartedly referred to foreign writers.

2

This short narrative begins with a full and detailed account of the entire life of Boris Ivanovich Pussikatov.

By profession Pussikatov was a musician. He was a member of a symphony orchestra where he played the musical triangle.

Perhaps a precise, specific name for this instrument exists, the author doesn't know, but be that as it may, the reader has surely had the opportunity to observe in the orchestra, way back and to the right, a stooping man with a somewhat pendulous jaw sitting next to a small iron triangle. This man, with a melancholy expression, tinkles his uncomplicated instrument in the appropriate places. Usually the conductor winks at him with his right eye for this purpose.

Some strange and amazing professions exist.

There are some professions that leave you dumfounded when you wonder how people came to practice them. How did it ever occur to people, say, to walk a tightrope, or whistle through their nose, or tinkle the musical triangle?

But the author is not making fun of his hero. No. Boris Ivanovich Pussikatov was decidedly not a bad person, not stupid, and he did have a secondary education.

Boris Ivanovich did not live in the city proper. He lived in the suburbs, in nature's bosom one might say.

Nature there wasn't anything to write home about, yet still, there were little gardens by each house, weeds, ditches, and wooden benches strewn with sunflower seed shells, and all this made the view attractive and pleasant.

In the spring it was absolutely charming.

Boris Ivanovich lived on Back Avenue in the house of Lukerya Fleasky.

Imagine, if you will, reader, a small wooden house painted yellow, a low rickety fence, a wide, yellowish gate leaning to one side. A yard. In the yard to your right is a small shed. A rake with broken teeth which has been there since the time of Catherine the Great. A cartwheel. A boulder in the middle of the yard. A porch with a torn-off bottom step.

And if you walk up onto the porch, you'll find a door lined with bast matting. Then the entrance hall, small, semi-dark, with a green barrel standing in the corner. On top of the barrel is a little plank. On the plank—a dipper.

Then there's a john with a thin, three-board-wide door. On the door is a piece of wood which can be turned to lock the door. A bit of glass serves as a window. There is a spider web on it. Right in the middle of the web is a plumpish spider.

Ah, a familiar picture dear to my heart.

All this was charming in its way as it reflected a quiet, dreary, and serene life. Even the busted step, in spite of its unbearably dreary appearance, to this day plunges the author into a quiet, meditative mood.

And every time Boris Ivanovich walked onto the porch, he looked at the broken-off crooked step, spat to one side in disgust, and shook his head.

Seven years ago Boris Ivanovich Pussikatov stepped for the first time onto the porch, for the first time crossed the threshold of this house, and for the first time uttered in a timid voice: "By the way, it wouldn't be here that there's a room for rent?''

The room for rent was precisely there. And precisely there Boris Ivanovich remained for the rest of his life.

He married his landlady, Lukerya Petrovna Fleasky. And he became the rightful owner of this entire estate.

The cartwheel, the shed, the rake, and the boulder—all this became his inalienable property.

It was with a worried smile that Lukerya Petrovna watched Boris Ivanovich become the owner of all this.

And when miffed, she never failed to scold Pussikatov and take him down a peg or two by saying that on his own he wouldn't have a shirt on his back or a roof over his head, and that he was the beneficiary of her many generosities.

Boris Ivanovich, though upset, said nothing.

He had grown fond of this house. And he had grown fond of the yard with the boulder. He had, in those seven years, indeed grown fond of living there.

There are people, you see, whose entire life with everything that has surrounded their life, from the first senseless cry to the last days, can be told in ten minutes.

The author will attempt to do this. The author will try briefly, in ten minutes, but nevertheless omitting no detail, to tell about the entire life of Boris Ivanovich Pussikatov.

On the other hand, there's really nothing to tell.

His life ran its course gently and quietly.

And if his life were to be broken down into paragraphs, into certain stages on which his subsequent life was built, there'd be five or six such short periods.

Here we have Boris Ivanovich, after he completed high school, entering life. He is twenty. He has a cute mustache. And no definite plans. He attempts to become a doctor, a gynecologist and obstetrician. Then, after installing a doorbell in an apartment, he wants to be an electrician. A chance meeting with a friend, a musician at the municipal theater, decides his career. Boris Ivanovich Pussikatov becomes a musician.

And here he is at twenty-five. He is an experienced musician. He no longer devours the conductor with his eyes as he used to, fearing to strike his instrument at the wrong time. Now he hits his instrument somewhat nonchalantly, with his eyes half closed as befits an experienced and indispensable musician. He now senses where his place in life is. It would appear that he has found his calling and discovered the purpose of his existence.

He now lives at full throttle. He strolls down the boulevard. He visits dance halls. And there sometimes he flits like a butterfly across the dance floor wearing a blue M.C.'s ribbon on his lapel.

He falls in love with a nice-looking chorus girl. He calls her the sweetest and tenderest names. He goes on dates with her to the most romantic spots in town. He even wishes to marry her, and he tells her about it in a thin, high-pitched voice. She, however, considering his salary too measly, leaves him for the second violin.

Then, at the age of thirty, Boris Ivanovich exchanges his existence as a provincial social lion and inveterate lover for the quiet life.

He moves out of town and marries his landlady. And he's been living with her for seven years.

And now, at thirty-seven, if he closes his eyes and thinks about the past, everything—the marriage, the revolution, the music, and the blue M.C.'s ribbon—everything blurs into a smooth, unbroken line.

Even his grand love blurs and turns into a kind of irksome memory, into a dreary joke about how the chorus girl asked him to make her a present of a polished-leather handbag and how he put away a ruble at a time to collect the necessary sum.

This is how the man lived. And he lived like this until he was thirty-seven, up until that moment, that extraordinary event in his life for which he was fined twenty-five rubles in court. Up to the very adventure for the sake of which, as a matter of fact, the author has taken the chance to mess up a few sheets of paper and use up a small bottle of ink.

3

And so Boris Ivanovich Pussikatov reached the age of thirty-seven. It is quite likely he will go on living for a very long time. He is a man of robust health, sturdy, and large-boned. As for Boris Ivanovich's slight, barely noticeable limp, it is due to a bunion he acquired way back in the time of the tsars.

The bunion, however, didn't interfere with Boris Ivanovich's good life, and it proceeded on an even keel. And everything would have continued fine and dandy right along, and the scandalous event would never have happened, were it not for a certain concern which constantly gnawed at Boris Ivanovich's quiet life.

The author is referring here to a particular notion, an obsessive thought Boris Ivanovich mulled over for many years with a somewhat bitter and rancorous smirk. He was thinking about life's fortuitousness and the fundamental instability upon which our entire existence is based.

Boris Ivanovich once even brought up this subject in his circle of close friends. It was at his birthday party.

"It's so strange, folks," said Boris Ivanovich. "Everything in life is somehow, you know, accidental. Everything, I am saying, is based on chance... I married Lusha, let's say... I'm not saying this because I'm unhappy or anything else like that at all. But it was an accident, just the same. I might have rented a room somewhere else altogether. It was an accident that I walked down this particular street... So what do we have? Accident!"

The friends reacted with lopsided grins, expecting a family clash. But no clash ensued. Lukerya Petrovna, showing true class, only walked out of the room rather ostentatiously, gulped down a dipperful of cold water, and returned to the table refreshed and cheerful. But that night, by contrast, she kicked up a row of such major proportions that the neighbors, who arrived on the run, tried to call the fire department out to take care of basic family relations.

After the row, however, Boris Ivanovich, lying on the sofa with his eyes open, continued to ponder his notion. He was reflecting that not just his marriage, but perhaps also his playing the triangle, and in general, his entire calling was simply an accident, nothing but an assortment of life's little coincidences.

"But if it is an accident," Boris Ivanovich mused, "then it means that nothing in the world is durable. It means no stability of any kind. It means everything may change tomorrow."

The author has no wish to prove the validity of Boris Ivanovich's notions. But at first glance everything in our esteemed life does in fact appear to be irregular and accidental. Accidental birth, an accidental existence made up of silly and accidental circumstances, and accidental death. All this indeed compels you to reflect that everything is absurd, that there isn't a single strict, firm law here on earth.

Really, how can there be a strict law when everything changes before our eyes, everything waxes and wanes, beginning with the grandest things—from God and love to the lousiest of human inventions.

For example, many generations and even entire nations have been brought up on the premise that love exists, and God exists, and that, say, the tsar was some sort of inexplainable phenomenon.

But now, even a marginally capable philosopher can, with the greatest of ease, with one stroke of a pen, prove the opposite.

Or science. There at least everything appears to be awfully convincing and true, but if you look back, you'll see that science was wrong about everything, and everything changed from time to time, from the rotation of the earth to some kind of theory of relativity or other.

The author is a man lacking higher education and has a hard time dealing with exact chronological dates and proper names, and he would, therefore, rather not attempt any strictly documented arguments. But you, reader, can take his word for this—he is not out to fool you.

And so it is with everything in life; everything is accidental even in our miserable and dreary-to-tears life, everything is unstable and impermanent.

It is unlikely, of course, that Boris Ivanovich was thinking about all this. Although he was not a stupid man, and he did have a secondary education, he had not progressed enough to generalize from the scientific point of view.

And yet, on a pettier level even he couldn't help noticing some kind of sly flim-flam in his everyday existence.

Doubt had been planted in his mind when he was still young.

But now this doubt assumed the proportions of a conflagration.

One day, when he was coming home along Back Avenue, Boris Ivanovich almost bumped into a shady character wearing a brimmed hat.

The character stopped in front of Boris Ivanovich and in a starved voice asked for a handout.

Boris Ivanovich reached into his pocket, pulled out some change and gave it to the beggar. Then for some reason he took a good look at him.

The beggar became embarrassed, covered his throat with his hand as if apologizing for not having either a collar or a tie there. Then, in that same starved voice, the beggar said that he was a former member of the landed gentry who had been sentenced to death by firing squad for his political convictions, and that at one time he himself gave beggars silver by the handful, and now, because of the course of the new democratic life, he was forced to ask for handouts.

Boris Ivanovich began earnestly to interrogate the beggar, for he was very interested in the details of his life in those earlier days.

"Well, what can I say?" said the beggar, flattered by the attention. "I was a frightfully rich landowner, I was wallowing in money, and now, as you can see, indigence and starvation are my lot—ain't got nothin' to eat. Everything, my kind citizen, changes in life when the time comes."

Boris Ivanovich gave the fellow another coin and slowly headed home. He didn't feel sorry for him, but some sort of ill-defined uneasiness took hold of him.

"Everything changes in life when the time comes," mumbled the kindhearted Boris Ivanovich as he walked home.

At home Boris Ivanovich told his wife, Lukerya Petrovna, about this encounter, embellishing it here and there with colorful details of his own, such as, for example, about the landowner throwing gold at the beggars and even drawing blood occasionally when hitting a beggar with a particularly hefty gold piece.

"So what," said she. "So he lived well, and now he doesn't. There isn't anything all that amazing in this. You don't have to go far—our neighbor has it plenty tough too."

And Lukerya Petrovna went on to tell about the former penmanship teacher, Ivan Semyonovich Kushakov, another one of life's losers. And he too had lived well at one time and even smoked cigars.

The story about the teacher also touched a sore spot in Pussikatov. He began questioning his wife about all the whys and wherefores of Kushakov's changing fortunes.

Boris Ivanovich even wanted to see this teacher. He immediately wanted to take a warm interest in his sorry life. And he started begging his wife, Lukerya Petrovna, to rush out at once, fetch the teacher and offer him tea.

Lukerya Petrovna bitched a little just to keep him in his place, called him "a lout," but nevertheless put on her kerchief and, burning with curiosity, set off to look for the teacher.

The teacher, Ivan Semyonovich Kushakov, arrived almost immediately.

He was a graying, dried-up little old man wearing a long shabby dress coat with no vest. His collarless dirty shirt bulged out on his chest like a lump. A single gaudy yellow brass cufflink incongruously thrust out its tinted glass head.

The graying stubble on the penmanship teacher's cheeks had

not been shaved in a long time and grew in clumps.

The teacher came into the room, rubbing his hands together and chewing something as he walked. Gravely, but almost cheerfully, he bowed to Pussikatov and for some reason winked.

Then he sat down at the table, pulled over the plate with the raisin bread, and began munching, chuckling quietly to himself.

When the teacher finished eating, Boris Ivanovich began to inquire avidly about his former life, and about how and why he had fallen so low as to walk around without a collar, in a dirty shirt, and wearing one bare cufflink.

The teacher, rubbing his hands and constantly winking cheerfully, but also spitefully, began by saying that indeed, he used to live pretty well, and even smoked cigars, but as the penmanship needs changed, and following the decree by the People's Commissars, this subject had been excluded from the curriculum.

"But now I'm used to it," the teacher said, "I don't mind it any more. And I am not complaining about my life. As for eating your raisin bread, that was out of habit and not from hunger at all."

Lukerya Petrovna, her hands folded on top of her apron, was splitting her sides with laughter feeling that the man was beginning to lay it on rather thick and before long he'd get to the real whoppers.

She looked at the teacher with unconcealed curiosity, expecting something quite extraordinary from him.

Boris Ivanovich, meanwhile, kept nodding his head and mumbling something as he listened to the teacher.

"That is how it is," said the teacher, again smiling without reason, "That's how everything in our lives changes. Today, say, they have abolished penmanship, tomorrow it'll be drawing, and then, before you know it, they'll give you the boot too."

"Come now, you don't mean that, do you," said Pussikatov choking a little. "How could they give me the boot... After all... Since I'm in the arts... If I play the triangle..."

"So what," said the teacher scornfully, "science and technology are marching forward. You just wait, they'll invent an electric... that instrument of yours, and it'll be curtains for you... You'll get the old boot, all right..."

Pussikatov, again choking slightly, looked at his wife.

"Nothing to it," said she, "particularly since science and technology are marching..."

Boris Ivanovich suddenly got up and began nervously pacing around the room.

"Well, so what, it's O.K. by me," he said, "I don't care!"

"It may be O.K. by you," said his wife, "but it's me who'll have to work my tail off. It's on my dumb shoulders that I'll be carrying you, you suffering Pilate!"

The teacher stirred in his chair and said in a conciliatory manner:

"And so it is with everything: today penmanship, tomorrow drawing... So, for instance, a man may live thinking that everything is durable. But, if you want to know the truth, everything in our life changes. Everything is insecure, my distinguished ladies and gentlemen."

Boris Ivanovich walked up to the teacher, said goodbye to him, and after inviting him to come to dinner—"let's say tomorrow"— volunteered to see the teacher to the door.

The teacher got up, took his leave and, rubbing his hands together cheerfully, said again as they went into the hallway:

"You can rest assured, young man, today penmanship, tomorrow drawing, and before long they'll zap you too."

Boris Ivanovich closed the door behind the teacher, went to the bedroom, and sat on the bed with his arms wrapped around his knees.

Lukerya Petrovna, wearing felt slippers with worn soles, entered the room and began readying it for the night.

"Today penmanship, tomorrow drawing," mumbled Boris Ivanovich, rocking gently on the bed. "And so it is with our whole life."

Lukerya Petrovna looked over her shoulder at her husband, spat peevishly on the floor without saying anything, and began to untangle her hair, which had become matted during the day, removing the straw and kindling lodged in it.

Boris Ivanovich looked at his wife and suddenly said in a melancholy voice:

"What do you think, Lusha, what if they do invent an electric one, the triangle, that is. They'd put, say, a little pushbutton on the podium... The conductor would push with his finger and it would ring..."

"Nothing to it at all," said Lukerya Petrovna. "Nothing to it... I'll be carrying you on my shoulders, I can tell... I can just feel you on my shoulders..."

Boris Ivanovich moved from the bed to a chair and became thoughtful.

"Makes you miserable, huh?" said Lukerya Petrovna. "Makes you think? Well, it's about time... If you didn't have a wife, and a house, where would a bare-assed bum like you go? Well, suppose, for example, they bounce you from the orchestra?"

"It isn't that they might bounce me, Lusha," said Boris Ivanovich. "It's that everything is so precarious. Chance... For some reason, Lusha, I play the triangle. And in general... If you take playing away from my life, how can I live? What else do I have to hang on to?"

Lukerya Petrovna lay in bed and listened to her husband, trying in vain to figure out the meaning of his words. And, presuming a personal insult in them, as well as a claim against her real estate, said again:

"I'll be carrying you on my shoulders, I can see it coming! I can, suffering Pilate you, you son of a biscuit."

"You won't," said Pussikatov.

And, choking again, he got up from the chair and began pacing up and down the room.

Terrible anxiety took hold of him. He ran his hand over his head as if attempting to sweep away some undefined thoughts, then sat down on the chair again.

And he sat in a motionless pose for a long time.

Afterwards, when Lukerya Petrovna's breathing changed into a gentle, slightly whistling snore, Boris Ivanovich left the room.

And, having found his hat, Boris Ivanovich stuck it on his head and, gripped by some extraordinary feeling of apprehension, walked out into the street.

4

It was only ten o'clock.

The still August evening was beautiful.

Pussikatov walked along the avenue swinging his arms wildly.

The strange and undefined anxiety had not left him.

He reached the railroad station, not even realizing that he was going there.

He made his way to the snack bar, drank a tankard of beer, and once more walked out into the street, again choking and feeling that he was out of breath.

Now he walked slowly, thinking about something with his head dejectedly bowed. But if you were to ask him what he was thinking about, he wouldn't have been able to answer you—he didn't know himself.

He kept on walking away from the station and when he reached the alley by the city park, sat down on a bench and took off his hat.

Some floozy with broad hips, wearing a short skirt and light-colored stockings, walked by Pussikatov, came back, walked by one more time, and finally, after giving him a look, sat down next to Pussikatov.

Boris Ivanovich started, glanced at the girl, jerked his head, and rapidly walked away.

And suddenly everything seemed awfully repulsive and unbearable to Pussikatov. And life as a whole seemed dreary and stupid.

"What in the world did I live for..." Boris Ivanovich mumbled. "When I arrive tomorrow, they'll tell me 'It's been invented. It has already been invented,' they'll say... 'It's been invented,' they'll say."

Boris Ivanovich's whole body was shaken by strong chills. He went forward almost at a run and when he reached the church fence he stopped. Then, after some groping, he opened the gate and went inside.

The cool air, several still birches, and the stone slabs over the graves had an immediate calming effect on him. He sat down on one of the tombstones and slipped into reverie. Then he said aloud:

"Today penmanship, tomorrow drawing. And so it is with our whole life."

Boris Ivanovich lit a cigarette and began wondering how he would live in case anything happened.

"Oh, I guess I'll survive," Boris Ivanovich mumbled, but I won't go back to Lusha. I'd sooner grovel before people. 'Behold citizens,' I'll say, 'a man is perishing,' I'll say. 'Don't abandon him in his misfortune...' "

Boris Ivanovich started and stood up. Again tremors and chills overwhelmed his body.

And suddenly Boris Ivanovich felt that the electric triangle had long since been invented but not revealed, so that this terrible secret could be used to crush him with one blow.

Overtaken by some sort of anguish, Boris Ivanovich left the church yard almost at a run and then began to walk down the street rapidly, scuffing his feet.

The street was quiet.

A few belated pedestrians hurried home.

Boris Ivanovich stood on the corner for a little while, then, almost without realizing what he was doing, walked up to a passerby, took off his hat, and said in a muffled voice:

"Citizen... Can you spare a kopeck..? A man is possibly perishing at this moment..."

The passerby, frightened, looked at Pussikatov and quickly walked away.

"A-a," shouted Boris Ivanovich, dropping gently down to the wooden sidewalk. "Citizens!.. Can you spare..? For my misfortune... For my misery..."

Several people surrounded Boris Ivanovich, looking at him with fright and astonishment.

The policeman on the beat, uneasily patting his leather gun holster with his hand, came over and tugged at Boris Ivanovich's shoulder.

"It's a drunk," somebody in the crowd said delightedly. "What a devil, got sloshed, and it ain't even Sunday. Doggone, there ought to be a law!"

A crowd of gawkers surrounded Pussikatov. A couple of charitable souls tried to stand him up on his feet. Boris Ivanovich tore himself from their grasp and bounded away. The crowd parted. Boris Ivanovich looked around in bewilderment, gasped, and suddenly, without uttering a sound, ran off.

"Get his ass, men! Grab 'im!" somebody howled in a frenzied voice.

The policeman abruptly and piercingly blew his whistle. And the trill of the whistle stirred up the whole neighborhood.

Boris Ivanovich ran at an even rapid pace without looking back, his head pulled down between his shoulders.

Behind him, whooping and slapping the mud with their feet, ran the people.

Boris Ivanovich dashed around the corner, reached the church yard fence, and jumped over it.

"There he goes!" howled the same voice. "This way, boys! This way, cut 'im off! We'll get his ass..."

Boris Ivanovich ran up the church steps, gasped weakly as he looked back, and strained at the door.

The door gave way and opened, its rusty hinges squealing.

Boris Ivanovich ran inside.

For a second he stood motionless, then, clasping his head with his hands, rushed up an ancient, ramshackle, and creaky staircase.

"In here!" screamed the volunteer detective. "Get 'im guys! Hit 'im with everything you got!.."

Nearly a hundred passersby and local residents stampeded through the church yard and stormed the church. It was dark inside.

Then someone struck a match and lit a wax candle stub in a huge candleholder.

High bare walls and the pitiful church appurtenances were suddenly illuminated by the faint flickering yellow light.

Boris Ivanovich was not in the church.

And when the crowd, pushing and buzzing, rushed back in some sort of terror, high up in the belfry the reverberating church bells began sounding the alarm.

The strokes, infrequent at first, grew closer and closer together and wafted through the night air.

It was Boris Ivanovich Pussikatov. Swinging the heavy brass clapper with great difficulty, he was ringing the bell as if he intended to awaken the whole town, all of the people.

This lasted a minute.

Then the howling of the familiar voice was heard again:

"There he is! Fellas! We ain't gonna let 'im get away, right? Everybody up the belfry! Get the bum!"

Several people rushed up.

When they brought Boris Ivanovich out of the church, there, by the church fence, was a huge crowd of partly dressed people, a detachment of police, and the suburban fire brigade.

Boris Ivanovich, held by the arms, was silently led through the crowd and hauled off to police headquarters.

Boris Ivanovich was deathly pale and his whole body trembled. His feet would not obey him and dragged behind along the pavement.

5

Eventually, many days later, when Boris Ivanovich was asked why he did all this, and most of all, why he climbed the belfry and started tolling, he shrugged his shoulders and angrily refused to speak: or else said that he didn't remember all the details. But when the details were supplied, he embarrassedly waved his hands, begging everyone not to talk about it.

That night they held Boris Ivanovich at the police station until morning. They drew up an unintelligible and nebulous complaint against him and let him go after making him sign an agreement not to leave town.

In his torn coat, without a hat, crestfallen and yellow, he returned home in the morning.

Lukerya Petrovna was wailing loudly and beating her breast, cursing the day she was born and her entire ever-so-miserable life with such human dregs as Boris Ivanovich Pussikatov.

Yet that same evening Boris Ivanovich, as always wearing a clean, neat coat, sat in the back of the orchestra and, with a melancholy expression, tinked his triangle.

Boris Ivanovich was, as always, neat and combed, and nothing about him showed what a terrible night he had lived through.

Only, two deep furrows from his nose to the lips were etched on his face.

These furrows hadn't been there before.

And the stooped posture Boris Ivanovich now assumed as he sat in the orchestra also hadn't been there before.

But it will all be water under the bridge.

Boris Ivanovich still has a long life to live.

What the Nightingale Sang about

They'll have quite a laugh at us some three hundred years from now, won't they? What a strange life those miserable people lived, they'll say. They had something called money, they'll say, passports. Something called vital statistics and square meters of living space...

Well, it's okay by me, let 'em laugh.

One thing bothers me, though: half of it they won't understand, the bastards. And how could they understand? They'll be living the kind of life we don't dream about, probably, in our wildest dreams.

The author doesn't know and doesn't intend to venture guesses about the kind of life they'll have. Why should the author frazzle his nerves and upset his health for no good reason, since he will never set foot in that wonderful life?

And anyway, it's not at all certain that it will be wonderful. The author expects, for his own peace of mind, that there will be a lot of junk and nonsense there too.

Still—it's possible the nonsense will be of the small variety. Let's say, if you'll pardon my paucity of speculation, someone's bald spot gets spat on from a dirigible. Or the folks at the crematorium get the orders mixed up, so that instead of the dearly departed's ashes, they'll hand out someone else's inferior remains.

This, of course, can't be helped—there'll always be these small-scale annoyances on the petty level of everyday existence. The rest of that life to come, though, will most likely be **splendid and outstanding.**

It's even possible there will be no such thing as money. Maybe everything will be free, gratis. Maybe they'll try to give away fur coats or foulards at department stores...

"Here, take this excellent fur coat, citizen," they'll say.

And you just walk on by. Your pulse won't even quicken.

"Forget it, dear comrades," you'll say. "What the hell do I want your fur coat for? I've got six already."

Hot damn! How cheerful and attractive the author visualizes this future life to be!

But here we must stop and reflect. If you do rid life of its penny-ante money matters and mercenary motivations, what wondrous shapes life itself will assume! What excellent qualities human relationships will immediately acquire! And, for example, love. How splendidly, I bet, will this flower of human emotions bloom!

My goodness, what a life it will be, what a life! With what sweet joy the author contemplates it even from afar, even without the slightest guarantee that he'll be around to see any of it. But there it is—love . . .

About love in particular we must say a few things. After all, many scientists and Party people in general have a tendency to downgrade this feeling. Come on, they say, what do you mean—love? There's no such thing as love. And there never was. And, anyway, it's just a trivial matter of vital statistics, something like a funeral.

Now this is something the author cannot accept.

The author has no desire to make confessions to chance readers, nor does he wish to expose his intimate life to some critics he finds particularly unpleasant. Still, as he looks back and tries to sort things out, he remembers a girl from his teenage days. She had a sort of cute, milky-white dumb face, tiny hands, pitiful shoulders. What starry-eyed raptures the author went into over her! What emotional moments the author experienced when, brimming with noble sentiments, he fell to his knees and, like a fool, kissed the ground she had walked on.

Fifteen years have gone by and, at a time when the author's hair is turning gray due to various illnesses, the vicissitudes of life, and worries about the daily bread, when the author simply does not wish to tell lies, nor is there any reason for him to lie, and, finally, when the author wants to see life as it is, without any falsehood or embellishments, he still maintains, without fear of appearing a laughable leftover from the last century, that scientific and Party circles are making a big mistake in this matter.

The author has a sure thing in forecasting the merciless dressing-down that these lines about love will elicit from public figures.

"Your own sorry personality, comrade," they'll say, "is no example. Stop shoving our noses," they'll say, "into your amorous fooling around. Your personality," they'll say, "isn't consonant with the epoch and, now that you mention it, it's a sheer accident that it has survived to this day."

"D'you hear that? Sheer accident! Well, now, if I may beg to inquire, what do you mean 'sheer accident'? Are you suggesting I should throw myself under the wheels of a streetcar?"

"That's entirely up to you," they'll say. "Under the wheels or off a bridge, only it's a fact that your existence has no rational basis. Take a look," they'll say, "at simple, unspoiled people, and you'll see that they don't think the way you do at all."

Ha!—Forgive me, reader, this insignificant laugh. Recently the author read in *Pravda* about some minor tradesman, an apprentice barber, who bit off a female citizen's nose out of jealousy.

That's not love! Are you going to say this is something insignificant, like a fly turd? Are you going to say the nose was bitten off in pursuit of a taste sensation? Well, then go to hell! The author doesn't want to get upset and give himself ulcers. He still has to finish the story, make a trip to Moscow, and what's more, visit certain literary critics—something the author isn't looking forward to at all—begging them not to overexert themselves writing critical essays and reviews of this story.

And so, love.

Let everyone think whatever he wants to about this refined feeling. As to this author, while fully recognizing his own nonentity and inability to live and even, if you insist, damn it, let there be a streetcar lying in wait for him, this author still stands firm in his opinion.

All the author wants to do is tell the readers about a minor love episode which unfolded against the backdrop of our time. What, again, they'll say, minor episodes? Again, trifles from a dime novel? What's the matter with you, young man, they'll say, have you gone crazy? Who needs it, they'll say, on a cosmic scale?

The author openly and honestly asks:

"Don't interfere, comrades! Let a man express himself—for the sake of discussion, if nothing else."

2

Phew! How tough it is to write literature!

You sweat buckets while trying to hack your way through an impenetrable jungle.

And for what? For the sake of some love story concerning citizen Preseedkin. This man is no skin off the author's nose. The author didn't borrow money from him, and does not even share the same ideology.

To tell the truth, the author has a profoundly indifferent attitude toward him. And the author does not feel like depicting him in brilliant colors. What's more, the author doesn't even remember the face of this Preseedkin, Vassily Vassilevich, all that well.

As to the other characters involved one way or another in this tale, well, these other characters also attracted little notice as they passed through the author's field of vision. Except, I suppose, Lisochka Kupbordov, whom the author remembers for very special and, so to speak, subjective reasons.

But Mishka Kupbordov, her kid brother, member of the Komsomol, him I remember less well. He was an extremely insolent young lout and a bully. As to his looks, he was rather blondish and somewhat fat-faced.

The author does not feel like dwelling on those looks of his either. The kid is a teenager. I'll describe him and, by the time the book comes out, the son of a bitch will have grown a few inches— then go figure out which is the real Mishka Kupbordov. And where did that moustache come from if, at the time these events unfolded, he had none?

As to the old lady herself—Ma Kupbordov, so to speak, the reader is not likely to complain if we refrain from describing her altogether. Particularly since it's so hard to describe old ladies artistically. You've seen one old lady, you've seen them all. Who the devil can figure out what kind of old lady she is? And, anyway, who on earth needs a description of her, say, nose? A nose is a nose is a nose. And my detailed description of it will not make the reader's sojourn on this planet any easier.

Of course, the author would not have undertaken to write an artistic story if he possessed only scant and irrelevant information about the heroes. No, the author has sufficient information. For instance, the author can visualize their whole way of life quite vividly. The crummy little Kupbordov house—kind of dark, one story. On the wall facing the street it says "22". Above this number is a board on which an ax is painted. This is a fire-fighting provision. Should a fire break out in the neighborhood, the pictures tell who is supposed to bring what. The Kupbordovs are supposed to bring the ax. Only, do they have an ax? Bet you they don't ... Anyway, it's not the business of artistic literature to look into this and perhaps draw the attention of the county administration to it.

But the author can picture the entire inside of their house and its material inventory, furniture-wise, in pretty vivid detail... Three not too large rooms. Uneven floors. A Becker piano. A rather frightful one at that. But still playable. Furniture on the mangy side.

A sofa. A cat of undetermined gender on the sofa. A cheap clock under a glass bell on the mantelpiece. Dust on the bell. A dishonest murky mirror above it—it lies to your face. An enormous trunk smelling of moth balls and dead flies.

Citizens from the capital, I bet, would find living in these rooms no fun at all!

I bet it would be no fun at all for such a cosmopolitan citizen to walk into that kitchen of theirs, where wet laundry hangs on a cord. And the old lady fixes dinner at the stove. She might, for instance, be peeling potatoes, the peel curling up under her knife like a ribbon.

But the author doesn't want the reader to think that he is describing all these trifling trifles with affection and admiration. No way! There's nothing sweet or romantic in these trifling memories. The author knows such houses and kitchens only too well. He's seen them. And lived in them. For all you know, he still does. And there's nothing good to be said about them—it's misery, nothing but misery. Every time you walk into a kitchen like that, some wet piece of laundry slaps you in the kisser—it never misses. And you should be grateful if it is a respectable piece of apparel, for it could be, heaven forbid, a wet stocking or something. Having your face wiped with a wet stocking is rather repulsive, wouldn't you say? Yech! How nauseating!

Anyway, for reasons of no concern to artistic literature, this author had been in the Kupbordov house on several occasions. And the author was always amazed that in such dust, must, and banality there lived such an outstanding young lady—such a, if I may say so, lily of the valley and nasturtium as Lisochka Kupbordov.

The author is not all that impressed with humans. It is time, citizens, to renounce our senseless self-glorification. The author believes that if a slug can learn to live amid wet slime, why shouldn't a human being get used to living among damp laundry?

Still, the author always felt profoundly sorry for Lisochka Kupbordov.

About her, however, we will speak at length and in some detail at the proper time. Right now the author is compelled to say a few things about citizen Vassily Vassilevich Preseedkin. Whether he is politically sound. What his relation to the Kupbordovs is. And whether he's a relative of theirs or what.

No, he isn't; he just stumbled into their lives by accident.

The author has already warned the reader that this Preseedkin's face didn't stick in his memory all that well. Although, at the same time, when he closes his eyes, the author can see citizen Preseedkin as if in the flesh.

This Preseedkin always walked slowly, even thoughtfully. He kept his hands behind him. He blinked his eyelashes at an unbelievable rate. Furthermore, his posture was somewhat stooped, as if this Preseedkin were weighted down by the vicissitudes of life. As regards the heels of his shoes, Preseedkin tended to wear them all the way down, towards the inside of his feet.

As far as his education is concerned, he had the appearance of someone who had no less than eight years of prerevolutionary schooling.

His social background—unknown.

The man arrived from Moscow while the revolution was in full swing and he preferred to keep mum about himself.

And what he came for is not clear either. Was it because the chances for eating were better in the provinces? Or did he get restless sitting in one place and feel the lure of faraway exciting places and adventures? Who in hell can figure out how his mind worked? You can't crawl into every psychology.

Still, his feeling that chances of eating would be better in the provinces is the more likely reason. Therefore, at first Preseedkin kept walking around farmers' markets casting hungry glances at fresh loaves of bread and mountains of every kind of produce.

But, by the way, how he managed to eat at all remains for the author an unclear mystery. He might even have panhandled. Or, perhaps, he might even have collected stoppers from soda-pop and mineral water bottles. And afterwards sold them. There were, you know, desperate profiteers of this sort in town.

It was, however, obvious that the man had had a wretched life. Everything about him looked worn out, and he had begun to lose his hair. And he walked around apprehensively, looking over his shoulder all the time and dragging his feet. Eventually he even stopped blinking his eyes and gazed at the world with a fixed and joyless stare.

But later, due to some unelucidated cause, he started going uphill. And by the time the present love story unfolded, Preseedkin had a solid social standing, state employment, and a seventh rank salary plus bonuses.

And by now, Preseedkin had rounded out his figure to some extent, having replenished, so to speak, his depleted system with the sap of life and again, often and annoyingly, he began to blink his eyes as he had of old.

And he walked through the streets with the somewhat ponderous tread of a man percolating with life to the core and having a right to live, the tread of a man who knows his full worth.

And indeed, at the time of the about-to-be-narrated events, he cut an impressive figure of a man just under thirty-two years of age.

He took long and frequent strolls in the streets and, swinging his cane, he lopped off flowers, seeds, and even leaves along the way.

Sometimes he sat down on a bench on the avenue and smiled happily as he energetically filled his chest with air.

What he thought about and what exceptional ideas illuminated his brain at such moments—no one knows. Maybe he didn't think about anything. Maybe he was busy imbuing himself with the delight occasioned by his lawful existence. Or, most likely, he was thinking that he absolutely had to find another apartment.

And indeed: he lived at Hirsutov's. Hirsutov was a deacon of the Living Church, and Preseedkin, in view of his official position, was greatly worried about living in the home of a person politically contaminated to such an extent.

He had asked many times if anyone knew, for God's sake, of any apartment or room, be it ever so lousy, as he just couldn't stand to live any longer in the home of the practitioner of a certain cult.

And finally someone, out of the kindness of his heart, cooked up a deal for him concerning a small room—about ten square yards. This happened to be precisely in the house of the esteemed Kupbordovs.

Preseedkin moved in without delay. One day he looked the room over, the next morning, bright and early, he started moving, having hired Nikita the water carrier for logistic purposes.

The reverend deacon had no use whatsoever for this Preseedkin; nevertheless, his vague though no doubt noble feelings having apparently been wounded, he cursed something awful and even threatened to punch Preseedkin in the nose if he ever got the chance. And while Preseedkin was piling his stuff on the cart, the deacon stood at the window laughing a loud and phony laugh, wishing to express his total unconcern with the departure.

The deacon's better half, on the other hand, ran out from time to time and, tossing some article into the cart, yelled:

"Nobody's keeping you. Get lost. Good riddance to bad rubbish."

The assembled onlookers and neighbors enjoyed a good laugh as they hinted broadly at the love relations which were thought to exist between these two. The author isn't going to stick his neck out on this. He doesn't know. Nor does he wish to spread any unnecessary gossip in artistic literature.

3

The old lady Darya Vassilevna Kupbordov had no pecuniary motivation or even any particular need to rent the room to Preseedkin, Vassily Vassilevich. It was rather that she feared that the authorities, striving for a more efficient use of square footage in view of the critical housing shortage, might decide to squeeze the Kupbordov family by putting some uncouth and undesirable element in to live with them.

Preseedkin even took some little advantage of the situation. And, as he walked by the Becker piano, he looked at it askance and with displeasure commented that this instrument, generally speaking, was not at all needed and that he, Preseedkin, was himself a quiet man shaken by the vicissitudes of life, who had been at two fronts and been shelled by heavy artillery and hence could not stand unnecessary petit-bourgeois noise-makers.

The old lady, offended, said that this dear little piano had been with them for forty years and that just to cater to Preseedkinian whims, they couldn't break it to pieces or pull the strings and pedals out of it, particularly since Lisochka Kupbordov was studying to play the instrument and that the pursuit of such studies might be, for all he knew, Lisochka's main goal in life.

Preseedkin brushed the old lady off brusquely and announced that his comment had been made in the form of a tactful request and not at all in the manner of a strict order.

In reply to which the old lady, now extremely offended, burst into tears and was about to refuse him the room altogether, but then she reflected on the possibility of their square footage being invaded from another quarter.

Preseedkin moved in the next morning and spent all day, late into the night, groaning in his room as he set up and arranged everything to suit his cosmopolitan tastes.

Two or three days went by quietly and without any changes in his routine.

Preseedkin went to work, returned late, and for a long time shuffled around his room in his felt slippers. In the evening he would munch on something and, eventually, go to sleep, snoring slightly and making chirping noises through his nose.

Lisochka Kupbordov walked around these two days in a somewhat subdued state and many times questioned her mother, as well as Mishka Kupbordov, about what kind of person Preseedkin was in their opinion—did he smoke a pipe, for example, and did he ever in his life have anything to do with the Commissariat of the Navy.

Finally, on the third day, she saw Preseedkin for herself.

This happened early in the morning. Preseedkin, as usual, was getting ready to go to work.

He was walking in the hallway wearing a nightshirt with the collar unbuttoned. Suspenders dangled behind from his pants, flapping from side to side. He was walking slowly, holding a towel and some aromatic soap in one hand, while with the other he was smoothing down his hair, which had gotten mussed during the night.

She was standing in the kitchen tending to her household chores, starting up the samovar or chipping kindling off a dry log.

She gave a gentle cry when she saw him, and darted to one side, embarrassed at being seen in her untidy morning garb.

But Preseedkin, standing in the doorway, examined the young lady with some surprise and even ecstasy.

And he was right: that morning she looked very good indeed.

That youthful freshness of her slightly sleepy face. That careless cascade of blond hair. Her gently turned up nose. And her bright eyes. And her not too tall, but pleasingly plump figure. All of this made her unusually attractive.

This was the captivating casualness—I might even say sloppiness—of a Russian woman who hops up from her bed in the morning and, without taking the time to wash, wearing felt slippers on her bare feet, starts doing her work around the house.

The author, as a matter of fact, rather likes such women. He has no complaints about such women.

If you come right down to it, there is really nothing good about these overweight women with their lazy bedroom eyes. There is no liveliness in them, no vividness of temperament, and, finally, no coquetry in their manner. Take a look at one—she doesn't move much, wears soft slippers, her hair is uncombed . . . As a matter of fact, I guess they are pretty repulsive, all things considered. And yet . . .

It is a strange thing, reader!

Some doll-like cutie pie, one of those inventions of bourgeois Western culture, so to speak, doesn't at all fill the author's bill. She has this kind of hairdo, who in hell knows what kind, Greek or something—look, but don't touch. And if you do, there'll be no end of kicking and yelling. Her dress is something unreal—again, don't you dare touch it. You might rip it or soil it. Tell me, who needs this? What is the big attraction and how can one find existential joy in this?

When our kind of girl sits down, for instance, everyone can plainly see that it is a girl sitting there and not a butterfly stuck on a pin. That's what those others are like—butterflies on a pin. Who needs it?

The author admires many things in foreign cultures; with respect to women, however, the author will cling to his national opinion.

It would seem that this is the kind of woman Preseedkin liked too.

In any event, he now stood in front of Lisochka Kupbordov and, with his mouth slightly agape from ecstasy, and without gathering in his dangling suspenders, he looked at her in joyful surpise.

But this lasted only a moment. Lisochka Kupbordov softly said, ''oh!'', scurried about the kitchen in a panic, then left, arranging her clothes and tousled hair along the way.

Towards evening, when Preseedkin came back from work, he walked to his room slowly, expecting to meet Lisochka in the hallway. But he didn't.

Even farther towards evening, therefore, Preseedkin made five or six trips to the kitchen and finally met Lisochka Kupbordov, whom he then greeted with an exceedingly respectful and courtly bow, tilting his head to one side and making with his hands a certain indefinite gesture which by convention shows rapture and unmitigated agreeableness.

Several days of such meetings in the hallway and in the kitchen drew them considerably closer.

Preseedkin nowadays returned home and, listening to Lisochka playing some plinkety-plunk on the piano, begged her to interpret more and more mushy tunes.

And she would play something like chopsticks or a Charleston, or strike a few bouncy chords from the Second, Third, or—who the hell can tell them apart?—even the Fourth of Liszt's rhapsodies.

And he, Preseedkin, who had twice been to all the fronts and been shelled by heavy artillery, listened to the clinking sounds of the Becker piano as if for the first time. And, sitting in his room, he dreamily leaned back in his armchair, thinking about the charms of human existence.

Mishka Kupbordov began living a life of great opulence. Twice Preseedkin gave him ten kopeks and another time fifteen with the request that Mishka whistle softly between his fingers when the old lady was in her kitchen and Lisochka alone in the room.

Why Preseedkin felt he needed to do this is extremely unclear to the author. The old lady looked on the love birds with perfect delight, calculating that she'd have them wed no later than fall and get Lisochka off her hands.

Mishka Kupbordov didn't go into the intricacies of Preseedkin's psychology either and whistled for all he was worth as many as six times a day, inviting Preseedkin to drift now into this room, now into that.

And Preseedkin duly went to that room, sat next to Lisochka, exchanged at first insignificant phrases with her, then asked her to play one of her very favorite pieces on the instrument. And there, by the piano, when Lisochka stopped playing, Preseedkin placed the gnarled fingers of a man in a philosophical mood—one who was seething with life and had been shelled by heavy artillery—on Lisochka's white hands and asked the young lady to tell him about her life, being eagerly interested in the details of her former existence. Sometimes, however, he would ask her whether she had ever felt the flutterings of true love before, or was this the first time.

And the young lady would smile enigmatically and, as she ran her fingers over the keyboard, she would say:

"I don't know..."

4

They fell passionately and dreamily in love.

Tears and trepidations marked their every meeting.

And each time they saw each other, they experienced afresh a new onrush of exalted joy.

Preseedkin, though, was even somewhat frightened as he peered into his soul and realized with amazement that he, who had twice been on all the fronts and who had earned the right to existence with such incredible difficulty, would now readily give up that life for one insignificant whim of this relatively cute young lady.

And, as he reviewed in his mind the women who had come into his life, including even the last one, the deaconess with whom he had, after all, had a romance (the author is completely convinced of it), Preseedkin thought with complete confidence that it was only now, in his thirty-second year that he had discovered true love and the genuine fluttering of that feeling.

Whether it was that Preseedkin was filled to the point of bursting with the sap of life or whether a human being has a predisposition and penchant for abstract romantic emotions remains for the time being a mystery of nature.

Be that as it may, Preseedkin could see that he was now a different man than he had been before, and that the composition of his blood had changed, and that all of life was laughable and insignificant before such extraordinary intensity of love.

And Preseedkin, this slightly cynical man, seething with life, who had been stunned by shells and who had more than once looked death in the face—well, this frightful Preseedkin even took a modest fling at poetry and wrote a dozen poems of various kinds and one ballad.

The author is not too familiar with his verse efforts but one poem, entitled "For Her, for That One...," which Preseedkin sent off to the *Dictatorship of Labor* and which was rejected by the editorial board as not being consonant with the socialist epoch, accidentally and thanks to the kindness of the technical secretary, Ivan Abramovich Krantz, was made known to the author.

The author has his own definite opinions about rhyme-mongering and amateur poetry and so the author will not burden the readers and typesetters with the entire and rather lengthy poem. The author submits to the attention of the typesetters only a couple of the last, most resounding stanzas:

> His flaming heart was eager to embrace
> Great love, for love and progress he equated.
> The lovely image of your dainty face
> Adoringly he always contemplated.
>
> Oh, Lisa, in the book of fates it's written
> The fellow who is hopelessly thus smitten
>   None other is but I.

From the point of view of the Formal Method, these verses may appear to be not all that bad. But, all things considered, these are pretty crummy verses and, indeed, are neither consonant nor co-rhythmical with the epoch.

Subsequently, Preseedkin lost interest in poetry and did not follow the thorny path of the poet. Preseedkin, always somewhat prone to Americanism, soon abandoned his literary achievements and buried his talents in his backyard without any regrets, and returned to his former life without projecting any more mad thoughts onto paper.

Preseedkin and Lisochka, who now met every evening, would leave the house and wander through the empty streets and boulevards well into the night. Sometimes they would go down to the river and there sit at the edge of a sandy cliff and watch with deep and silent joy the rapid waters of the Grasshopper River. At other times, however, holding each other by the hand, they softly uttered exclamations of delight and engaged in ecstasies spawned by the unbelievable colors of nature or a whispy airy cloud racing across the sky.

All this was new to them, charming and—most important—it seemed to them that they were seeing everything for the first time.

Sometimes the couple went to the country and walked in the woods. And there, holding one another by a finger, they walked around all mushy-eyed and, stopping in front of some pine tree or fir, they looked at it in wonderment, sincerely amazed at the daring and fanciful tricks of nature, which had produced from under the ground a tree so useful to man.

And then Vassily Preseedkin, shaken to the core by the unusualness of his existence on this earth, with its amazing laws, and overtaken by an excess of emotion, fell to his knees in front of the young lady and kissed the ground around her feet.

All the while everywhere around them, there was the moon, the mysteriousness of the night, grass, fireflies chirping, the silent forest, frogs and bugs. All around there was some sort of sweetness and appeasement in the air. All around was this kind of simple existence, which the author does not quite wish to renounce and therefore he cannot, in any shape or form, accept the notion that he is a superfluous figure on the stage of the new life at its sunrise. The author, just like every insignificant Boris, Ivan, or Sergei, thought himself well within his right to live out his life, however miserably, in spite of all the jeering of his severe and impatient critics.

And so, Preseedkin and Lisochka liked these out-of-town strolls best of all.

But during one such charming stroll, on a damp night one assumes, the careless Preseedkin got badly chilled and was soon quite ill. A disease akin to mumps forced him to stay in bed.

In the evening after the walk, Preseedkin felt a slight shiver and a piercing pain in this throat. Later that night his face began to balloon.

Crying softly, Lisa would come to his room and, her hair down, wearing soft slippers, she rushed from the bed to the table, not knowing how to proceed or what to do, wondering how to alleviate the lot of the patient.

Even Ma Kupbordov herself trundled into the room several times a day asking whether the patient would like some stewed rhubarb, which is supposedly unsurpassed for cases of infectious disease.

Two days later, when Preseedkin's kisser was bloated beyond all recognition, Lisochka fetched a doctor.

After examining the patient and prescribing some medicines, the doctor left, apparently cursing in his heart because he had been paid in small change.

Lisochka Kupbordov ran after the doctor, caught up with him in the street and, wringing her hands, began babbling and asking— Tell me the truth, doctor, is there any hope? And she let the physician know that she couldn't survive the loss of this man.

Thereupon the physician, accustomed by reason of his profession to such scenes, said with indifference that mumps is nothing but mumps and it seldom happens, unfortunately, that people die of it.

Somewhat peeved by the insignificance of the danger, Lisochka sadly returned home and began self-sacrificingly to look after the patient, not sparing her health or her feeble efforts, not even fearing to catch this disease that makes one look like a hog.

The first few days Preseedkin was afraid to lift his head from the pillow and, feeling his swollen neck with his gnarled fingers, kept asking whether Lisochka Kupbordov would stop loving him after his illness, which had made it possible for her to see him in such a disfigured and repulsive state.

But the young lady, begging him not to worry, kept saying that, in her view, he had become an even more imposing representative of his sex than he had been before.

And Preseedkin laughed softly and said gratefully that this illness had more than anything else, tested the endurance of their love.

5

It was an absolutely extraordinary love.

Furthermore, ever since he got up from his bed of pain, and his head and neck had once again assumed their former shapes, he began to believe that Lisochka Kupbordov had saved him from certain death.

Because of this, to their love relationship was now added a certain solemnity and even generosity.

One day, very soon after his illness, Preseedkin took Lisochka by the hand and in the voice of a man who has come to a decision about something, asked her to hear him out without asking any unnecessary questions for the time being, and without butting in with any of her silly lines.

Preseedkin made a long and solemn speech about the fact that he knew to perfection what life was and he knew how difficult it was to exist on earth and that before, when he was still a wet-eared youth, his attitude toward life had been criminally frivolous, something that caused him a lot of suffering at one time, but now that he had gone over the high-water mark of thirty and had been wisened up by life's experiences, he knew how to live and knew the unforgiving and unshakeable laws of life. And that, having thought all this over, he expected to introduce certain changes into the draft of his future life.

In a word, Preseedkin made Lisochka Kupbordov a formal proposal of marriage, insisting that she need not worry about her future wellbeing, even if Lisochka Kupbordov persisted in being unemployed and would not be in any position to contribute her fair share to the modest Preseedkin family kettle.

After hemming and hawing a little and talking about free love for the sake of gilding the lily or in order to give this heartfelt moment a tinge of elegance, Lisochka nevertheless accepted the proposal, adding that she'd been waiting for it for a long time and that had he not made it, he would have been the worst scoundrel and bum. As to free relations, they too are fine and excellent at the proper time but it's not at all the same thing and one was definitely not the other.

With this happy news, Lisochka Kupbordov ran at once to her Ma and also to the neighbors, asking them to come to the nuptials which would take place within a very short period of time and would be endowed with a modest and family character.

The neighbors warmly congratulated her, saying that it was high time, and that she had certainly endured the hopelessness of her existence long enough.

Ma Kupbordov, of course, shed a few tears and went to look for Preseedkin to confirm for herself the reliability of these facts.

And Preseedkin reassured the old lady by solemnly asking for permission to henceforth call her "Ma." The old lady, crying and blowing her nose into her apron, said that she'd been living in this world for fifty-three years but that this day was the happiest day of her life. And, in turn, she asked to call him Vassya. Preseedkin generously gave his consent to this.

As far as Mishka Kupbordov is concerned, Mishka took the change in the life of his sister rather indifferently and presently was running through the streets somewhere at a breakneck speed, like a bat out of hell.

Now the love birds didn't go out of town any more. Most of the time they stayed at home and, prattling late into the night, discussed plans for their future life.

During one such conversation, Preseedkin, pencil in hand, began to draw on paper the layout of their future rooms, which would constitute something like a separate small, but cozy, little apartment.

Arguing themselves out of breath, they tried to prove to each other what the best place for the bed was, and where the table should be, and where they should put the dresser.

Preseedkin was trying to convince Lisochka not to be so stupid as to put the dresser in a corner.

"Putting the dresser in a corner is extremely lower middle class," he said. "Every Miss Nobody puts it there. It's infinitely better and more monumental to put the chest of drawers in the corner and cover it with a lace scarf which Ma, I trust, won't begrudge to give us."

"Having a chest of drawers in the corner is extremely low middle class too," said Lisochka, almost in tears. "Besides, the chest of drawers is Ma's, and whether she'll let us have it or not is still a question to be asked and answered."

"Baloney," said Preseedkin, "what do you mean, 'she won't let us have it?' We can't keep our linen on window sills, can we? It's obvious nonsense."

"You, Vassya, talk to Ma about it," Lisochka said sternly. "Simply talk to her as if she were your own mother. Say—'Give us the chest of drawers, Mommy dear.' "

"Nonsense," said Preseedkin. "On the other hand, I can go

right now and see the old lady if that's what you want."

And Preseedkin went to the old lady's room.

It was now pretty late. The old lady was asleep.

Preseedkin shook her for a long time, but she just kicked in her sleep and refused to wake up and understand what was expected of her.

"Come on, Ma, wake up," Preseedkin said sternly. "Can't Lisochka and I, after all, expect some little comfort? We can't have our linen gathering dust on window sills, now can we?"

Barely understanding what was going on, the old lady launched into a spiel to the effect that the chest had been standing in its rightful place for fifty-one years and that now, in the fifty-second year, she had no intention of dragging it around this way and that and tossing it at the first person who came along. Also, she didn't make chests of drawers herself. And it was a bit late for her, in her old age, to start learning the carpenter's craft. It was about time people understood this and quit making an old lady miserable.

Preseedkin set about to shame Ma, saying that, as a person who'd been at all the fronts and had been shelled twice by heavy artillery, he should be able, shouldn't he, to expect, at last, a peaceful life.

"Shame on you, Ma!" Preseedkin said. "You're being stingy about that chest of drawers. And you can't take it to the grave, you know. I want you to realize that."

"I won't give up my chest of drawers!" the old lady said in her high-pitched voice. "When I die, you can take every stick of furniture for all I care."

"Yeah, sure. When you die!" said Preseedkin indignantly. "I should live so long!"

Seeing that things were taking a serious turn, the old lady wasted no time going into a fit of wailing and whimpering, but still managed to say that, all things considered, the last word should come out of the babe's mouth belonging to her innocent child Mishka Kupbordov, particularly since he was the only male representative of the Kupbordov clan and the chest of drawers belonged by rights to him, not to Lisochka.

Mishka Kupbordov, after being awakened, was extremely unwilling to give up the chest of drawers.

"Yeah," said Mishka. "He shells out a lousy ten kopeks and now he wants the chest of drawers. Chests of drawers are worth money, you know."

Preseedkin then slammed the door and went back to his room where he bitterly upbraided Lisochka, saying that being without a chest of drawers is like being without a right arm and that he, a man tempered in battles, knew what life was like and would not retreat from his ideals one single step.

Lisochka literally bounced from Preseedkin to her mother and then back again, imploring them to come to some kind of agreement and suggesting that every once in a while the chest of drawers be shuttled from one room to the other.

Then, asking Lisochka to quit bouncing back and forth, Preseedkin suggested that she go to bed and gather her strength the better to tackle this life-or-death problem the next morning.

The morning brought nothing good.

Many a bitter and insulting truth was uttered on all sides.

The angered old lady said with desperate resoluteness that she had him, Vassily Vassilevich Preseedkin, figured out up one side and down the other, and that while today he was demanding the chest of drawers, tomorrow he'd make mincemeat pie out of her and eat it along with his vegetables. That's the kind of man he was!

Preseedkin shouted that he'd swear out a complaint to the police and have her arrested for maliciously disseminating false and slanderous rumors.

Lisochka, shrieking softly, scurried from one to the other, beseeching them to quit yelling already and try to examine the problem calmly.

The old lady then said that she had outgrown the age when people yell and that she could, without yelling, tell all and sundry that Preseedkin had, during this time, had dinner with them three times and hadn't even bothered, as a good-will gesture, to offer any compensation whatsoever for even one of those dinners.

Terribly excited, Preseedkin acidly said that in exchange he had, while walking with Lisochka, many times bought her caramels and gumdrops and twice a bouquet of flowers and nonetheless, he was submitting no bills to Ma Kupbordov. To which Lisochka, biting her lips, said that he should not lie so shamelessly, that there had been no gumdrops, just a couple of fruit losenges and a small bunch of violets not worth half a kopek, which, to boot, withered the very next day.

After saying this, Lisochka left the room crying, leaving everything in the hands of fate.

Preseedkin wanted to run after her and apologize for supplying inaccurate information but, again locking horns with the old lady, he called her "Ma Hellhound," spat at her, and ran out of the house.

For two days Preseedkin was gone no one knew where. And when he reappeared, he announced in a formal tone of voice that he no longer deemed it possible to reside in the Kupbordov house.

Two days later, Preseedkin moved to an apartment in the Skinsky house. All four days Lisochka made it a point to stay in her room.

The author doesn't know the details of Preseedkin's moving, nor does he know what bitter moments Lisochka experienced. Nor, indeed, that she experienced any at all. Nor whether Preseedkin was sorry about the whole thing or whether he had acted with full awareness and determination.

The author has only gathered that Preseedkin, after moving, kept on visiting Lisochka Kupbordov for a long time, having, it is true, married Marussya Skinsky in the meantime. And the two of them, still reeling from their misfortune, sat side by side exchanging insignificant words. At times, however, as they sifted through their memories and came up with a particularly happy episode or occurrence from the past, they talked about it with sad and pitiful smiles, holding back tears.

Occasionally Lisochka's mother came into the room and then all three of them deplored their fate together.

Eventually Preseedkin stopped visiting the Kupbordovs. And, when he met Lisochka in the street, he greeted her correctly and with reserve and then continued on his way...

6

That's how this love ended.

At another time, of course, maybe some three hundred years into the future, this love story would not have ended this way. It would have bloomed, my dear reader, splendidly and extraordinarily. But each lifetime imposes its own rules.

To conclude this narrative, the author wants to say that as he was unfolding this uncomplicated story of love, he was caught up in the emotional upheavals of his heroes and completely lost sight of the nightingale which was mentioned so mysteriously in the title.

The author fears that the honest reader or typesetter, or maybe even a hopeless critic, might be upset after reading this story.

"Wait a minute," he'll say, "what about the nightingale? What's the idea, trying to hornswoggle your readers," he'll say, "and entice them with a frivolous title?"

It would, of course, be absurd to start the story of this love all over again. This is not at all what the author is trying to do. The author only wants to recall certain details.

This occurred when the flame of their feeling was burning at its brightest, when it had reached its highest point—at the time Preseedkin and the young lady went out of town and strolled through the woods until after dark. And there, as they listened to the chirping of bugs or the singing of a nightingale, they would stand motionlessly transported for a long time. And then Lisochka, wringing her hands, asked many a time:

"Vassya, what do you think this nightingale is singing about?"

To which Vassya Preseedkin replied without undue sentimentality:

"His belly's empty, so he sings."

And only later, when he had familiarized himself a little with the young lady's psychology, Preseedkin answered in greater detail and more vaguely. He suggested that the bird was singing about some future many-splendored life.

That's precisely what the author thinks. The nightingale was singing about a wonderful future life maybe some three hundred years from now, or, perhaps, even less.

Yes, reader, let those three hundred years pass by quickly, like a dream, and then we'll really start to live!

If, however, things are bad then too, the author, his heart cold and empty, will agree to consider himself a superfluous figure on the backdrop of the rising life.

Then he won't mind throwing himself under the wheels of a streetcar.